AF580893

SUCH WOMEN ARE DEADLY

By the same author

FACT

They Challenged the Yard
When Killers Err
Clues that Spelled Guilty
Hands of Terror
Murders Most Strange
Great Detective Exploits
Famous Judges and Their Trials
Triumphs of Scotland Yard
Adventures in Murder
Famous Manhunts

FICTION

Heads You Die
Wantons Die Hard
Don't Argue with Death
Stand-in for Murder
Superintendent Slade Investigates
Death Pays the Piper
The Inverted Crime
She Died Laughing
Murder Out of Season
The Glass Alibi
The Frightened Chameleon
Hangman's Moon
Atomic Murder
The Arsenal Stadium Mystery
Tragedy in E Flat
The Secret of Tangles

SUCH WOMEN ARE DEADLY

Leonard Gribble

JOHN LONG
London

JOHN LONG LIMITED
178–202 Great Portland Street, London, W.1

AN IMPRINT OF THE  HUTCHINSON GROUP

London Melbourne Sydney
Auckland Bombay Toronto
Johannesburg New York

First published 1965

© Leonard Gribble 1965

This book has been set in Imprint, printed in Great Britain on Antique Wove paper by The Anchor Press, Ltd., and bound by Wm. Brendon & Son Ltd., both of Tiptree, Essex.

For

MARY MASH

the nicest woman I never met
. . . if she knows what I mean.
And she does!

Contents

Author's Preface 9

1 Nemesis in the Nude 13
[*Simone Deschamps*]

2 Double for Murder 26
[*Augusta Fullam*]

3 The Chocolate Killer 39
[*Christiana Edmunds*]

4 The Shotgun Divorce 53
[*Addie Mae Lavespere*]

5 A Bride for Death 66
[*Grete Beier*]

6 Stronger than Love 80
[*Mary Blandy*]

7 Invitation to an Ogress 94
[*Jeanne Weber*]

8 Daughter of Hatred 107
[*Lizzie Borden*]

CONTENTS

9 Siren of Doom 121
[*Countess Tarnowska*]

10 Blows and Bullets with Love 134
[*Kitty Byron, Ruth Ellis*]

11 The Love Vampire 147
[*Jeanne Brécourt*]

12 The Mail Order Circe 161
[*Belle Gunness*]

Author's Preface

The late Mr. Kipling's assertion that 'the female of the species is more deadly than the male' may be considered by the cynical to be the masculine enthusiasm of an anti-feminist, although, in a negative way, it could be held to afford encouragement to the more subtle feminist! After all, we live in an age when the sexes boastfully tell each other, 'Anything you can do I can do better,' and when militant females are demonstrating a grim readiness and ability to storm the last strongholds of male privilege and isolation.

So it should not be surprising that the murderess, if only in deference to the Kipling axiom, should at least show from the broad social record that she can in a general narrative sense hold her own with a murderer in such basic matters as horrifying intention and savage single-mindedness of purpose.

In one respect, at least, the murderess has an advantage over a murderer, considered quite objectively.

For the woman who kills is almost always a creature of awe, even when she is repellent, and that cannot be said of a great many murderers whose names have become common in several senses. When a woman slays deliberately she is seen to be inverting her natural function of providing life, and it is probably as much for this reason, as for any lingering notion of her being a weaker creature than a man, that the conception of her choosing to employ violence seems somehow particularly unnatural and deplorable.

The women selected in this volume belonged to different races and to different times. Some were younger than the others, but their violence was just as deadly. They all had their reasons or motives. For gain, for hate, for revenge, for the temporary satiation of a blood lust, even in some twisted way for love. Their reasons or motives were not unique. All had been shared by other killers, men and women, but it is true that the women here had their own personal and particular circumstances which determined, very largely, when and where deadly violence erupted. Such circumstances can break the mould of character or reshape it. Therein lies the concentrated essence of drama and stark tragedy.

That is what these women reveal in the stories of their progress towards that violence which made their names notorious and has allowed their notoriety to live after them.

All reveal fascinating facets of the human species in those throes which prompt a resort to violence. Some were high-born, some well bred, some came from slums and were creatures who never truly cleansed themselves of the gutter's clinging filth. But all found a common sisterhood in their deliberate employment of destructive force, all destroyed other human beings.

Their motives are as varied as the clothes they wore. Perhaps the sociologist may be brash enough to attempt to draw some general conclusions from the net results of such violence as these women employed. That is not the purpose here.

Here it suffices that over a period of two hundred years sluts and ladies alike committed murder because they felt a compulsive urge towards that end, knowingly and understandingly, and were not deterred by any consideration of the terrible wages their sin might earn. For murder is both a sin and a crime. These women did not shrink enough to keep their hands and consciences clean. Some appear more cold-blooded than others, some evoke an uncomfortable feeling of compassion, others had a quality that even murders compassion.

But they all did these terrible acts, and they all chose deliberately to do them. For that reason alone they are assured of an abiding interest in the shape circumstances gave to their lives and sometimes to their loves.

For circumstances, extending through every hour from birth to burial, can conspire in such fashion against any who read these narratives of women who could not conform to a civilized code. There are harrowing scenes that were the products of their bitter nonconformity, and if the reader is aware of rising revulsion it is as well to remember the acts of these murderesses produced good as well as evil. For by their attempting to understand the motivations and compulsions of such women the sociologists of today have reached towards a more truthful appreciation of the human changes inherent in woman's social climb from chattel to equal.

It has been a truly steep climb.

Too steep for the women recorded here, who not only broke a code but tried a deadly short cut to appease their own private devils. And if society is plagued with fewer private devils today it is in part because these women and others like them lived and failed and left their failure as a grim legacy to the human race.

1 * Nemesis in the Nude

On the 15th of October, 1958, before the crowded court-room of the Seine Assize Court, Maître Fouquin, making his closing speech for the prosecution, turned from facing the presiding judge, Counsellor Bonhoure, to stare at the pale-faced woman in the dock, watching him with wide eyes.

'This is the wild beast,' Maître Fouquin declared, stabbing a forefinger at the prisoner. 'She killed Marie-Claire Evenou in the manner of a beast using its claws.'

Almost everyone in court that day, listening to the finely drawn mixture of horror and contempt blended in the prosecutor's voice, shuddered.

But Simone Deschamps did not shudder. She did not blink her wide eyes. Although she must have realized she was listening to the voice of her personal doom, she gave no sign. It was as though something inside her had died. Perhaps it had. Crushed by the weight of a new sanity that had come to her while listening in the past days to her own dreadful story, one that had blazoned her name across Europe as 'the demon lover'.

She was forty-eight, a woman whose life had touched no memorable height and sunk to no significant depth before she met Yves Evenou, and through the smoke rising from his cigarette saw his small dark eyes, with their feral glint, staring at her with interest.

To look back to that day she had to pierce the miasma created by five years of incredible folly. It was in 1953 that she sat in Dr. Yves Evenou's waiting-room, wondering how much she should tell the man of medicine, when she was summoned to his consulting-room. She was not a woman with pretensions to physical grace or beauty. Her face was thin, her hair was dark and rather lustreless, and she had little money to spare for good cosmetics or costly clothes. Not that she could not envy women who dressed to captivate susceptible males. Simone Deschamps was a dressmaker. Her fingers were deft with a needle. They knew the texture of good materials and had often lingered lovingly over a particularly well-turned hem or a well-nigh invisible seam that had the effect of making a garment she had made appear moulded to the feminine curves of its fortunate wearer.

She sat in the waiting-room turning her fingers, coarsened with countless needle pricks, over and over, wondering if it would be wiser to rise and leave before she incurred this expense she could not really afford, for to her a doctor was a luxury. She was still in two minds about staying or leaving when the door of the consulting-room opened, and Yves Evenou stood there looking at her, the half-smoked cigarette in the corner of his lean mouth with the bitterly twisted underlip, his balding head presenting an unnaturally high forehead, with two slits of dark eyes watching her.

He nodded to her, turned, and went back into the consulting-room, leaving the door open. She rose and entered after him. There was no longer any thought in her mind about leaving. When the door of the consulting-room closed after her a die had been cast.

Two curiously potent human forces had moved within the field of each other's deadly magnetism. How long the woman remained in the consulting-room is not known. It is not known, even, if she spoke to him about the malady that had brought her to the waiting-room. But it is certain that when she left Dr. Yves Evenou's consulting-room the first overture had been made in an evil bargain.

The next meeting was outside the consulting-room.

Yves Evenou's breath carried the sour-sweet odour of port wine. The hand he placed about the woman had possessive fingers. They ate in a restaurant, and he smoked throughout the meal, and his speech became slurred, which was just as well when it is remembered that Yves Evenou, under the influence of the port wine he imbibed so freely, had a foul tongue.

However, its foulness did not appear to contaminate his table companion. She listened to his suggestions, and far from finding them outrageous was attracted by their bestial tone. Yves Evenou was a man with degrading sexual instincts. Their appetite was sharpened by the wine he drank. He explained in his slurred speech what he could offer the woman for her sharing.

She opened her eyes wider and smiled.

So a man of medicine with a depraved mind met a woman who was prepared to accept that depravity and match it with her own inner craving for satiety.

The two evil forces were not only in each other's field of magnetism by this time. They had become inseparable and were flowing together.

Simone Deschamps, the dowdy dressmaker with dark sexual instincts that required satiating, had found the depraved lecher who could provide the demanding animalism that would make her a dutiful slave to desire.

She became the drunken doctor's mistress.

In its more public aspects the liaison was a shabby one. Evenou treated her badly. He was a brute who took baneful pride in displaying his brutishness. He bullied her when they sat in restaurants and mocked her in the hearing of stone-faced waiters. Upon occasions we are assured he even forced her to pay for their meals.

Yet such manifestations of dark power were merely means of assuring himself that she was his creature. That was apparently all-important to him. For Yves Evenou was a man with two separate and distinct personalities. At home, if he was not the loving husband a Frenchwoman could naturally expect in the man she had married, certainly Marie-Claire Evenou found no reason to complain to her close friends, for Yves appeared to be a devoted father to their daughter Françoise, who was twelve.

But away from his wife and out of his consulting-room Dr. Evenou was a creature obsessed with the brooding dictates of his baser nature. He demanded dark satisfactions he could not morally claim from his legal wife. He came to demand them from Simone Deschamps.

As their association continued she came to satisfy those demands in ways that reached the extreme in moral degradation and the total destruction of self-respect.

They indulged in what came to be described in print as 'sadistic orgies'. In time satiety demanded other expressions of the woman's sexual submissiveness to the demanding male. Evenou came to his mistress's room accompanied by Algerians, and when he told her to make love to them she complied, while he watched the performance like a perverted priest overseeing some satyric rite.

He introduced her to flagellation. She submitted to his callous insistence.

He forced her to undertake semi-public strip-tease acts. Again she offered no opposition to his growing demands. Month by month the bond between these two depraved lovers became braided into shackles from which neither could break free, not the man because he had no desire, not the woman because she had lost her last semblance of will.

His orgiastic demands, to which she was invariably the acquiescent partner, moved with terrible logic towards a culminating violence. Every depraved act of these so-called demon lovers was a step towards an eventual act which would climax their sordid relationship with overwhelming disaster.

Yet Yves Evenou, throughout this period of moral decay, continued to turn two faces towards the world.

One of his female patients later declared he was 'a gentle and a charming man'.

Another said, 'He used to tell me that his wife was a saint on earth.'

A neighbour firmly believed that Yves Evenou was passionately devoted to his daughter.

'He was always kind to his wife,' insisted a friend of the family.

But Madame Porrée was a shrewder person. She saw beneath the veneer and behind the façade of the respectable doctor who laboured to assuage the ills and pains of his fellows. She was almost vehement in her denunciation of the man who had lost her respect.

'He was a depraved creature,' she declared bitterly.

True, at the time she could have been viewing a man brought

low by his wanton excesses with some measure of hindsight, but her words have a ring of conviction.

'I used to call him Dr. Port Wine,' she admitted, 'because he drank so much of it.'

Well, she was in a position to know, for she was the proprietor of a restaurant where Evenou and his sad-faced mistress frequently ate an evening meal.

'He used such disgusting language,' Madame Porrée added, 'that I have had to send a young waitress out of the room. And as to that Simone Deschamps—well, he treated her like dirt. She was absolutely dominated by him.'

It was the observant and disapproving restaurant proprietor who reported that upon occasion the doctor mockingly told his mistress to pay for their meal.

It was at Madame Porrée's restaurant that Yves Evenou and Simone Deschamps had a meal on the day the drunkard dreamed up a way of forcing Simone Deschamps to commit the last act that would make her his creature beyond redemption. These incredible lovers had brought themselves to discussion of murder.

The victim was to be Madame Evenou.

She was sick, and had been an invalid for some considerable time. Her death was to be a sacrifice to their own perverted passion, and the crime was to be enacted in the name of love that was a mockery of all human tenderness.

It was during the lunch at Madame Porrée's that Simone Deschamps learned she and her perverted lover had come to a crucial crossroads in their depraved association. Indeed, she must have been prepared for his ultimatum, for they had been progressing with harsh logic towards the eventual elimination of Madame Evenou. Simone Deschamps had moved into the block of flats in the Avenue des Allies where the Evenous had an apartment on the first floor.

'I want you where I can get at you when I want to get at you,' Evenou had said with characteristic lack of subtlety.

Simone Deschamps had moved into a ground-floor flat, the cost of which strained her resources.

Thereafter the love sessions of this strange pair became more frequent, and with proximity Evenou became even more demanding. Their wayward passion was indulged in the knowledge that the unsuspecting wife sat in a room or lay sleeping just above their heads.

There were times when the ailing Madame Evenou appeared to take a turn for the better, and under the medical treatment of her husband her health gave no sign of recovering its lost bloom with any degree of permanence. For the truth was the sadistic husband took pleasure from his wife's physical helplessness.

Until contemplation of her helplessness palled. That was when he decided he had to be freed of her presence in his home. His wife must be removed by his mistress. That was the ultimatum he gave Simone Deschamps across the lunch table in Madame Porrée's restaurant.

'We can't go on,' he said, 'unless she is removed. You must remove her. You have taken her place. You have a duty to me.'

This was the kind of distorted argument that had helped to make the woman with the large eyes and slightly bent nose his chattel.

'Marie-Claire must die today,' he insisted. 'You must kill her. I will make preparations of course. I shall see that everything is made ready. I think it would be as well if you stabbed her. Yes, that would be best,' he added dreamily, a happy man at the thought of his wife's blood being shed.

The meal had not been finished when Simone Deschamps, after much whispering across the table, rose and left the restaurant. Evenou lit a cigarette and waited. He presented the picture of a man with time on his hands, a man who could afford not to become impatient. He smoked and smiled contemplatively and sipped his wine, which, each time he held the glass level with his eyes, looked so much like blood.

Twenty minutes passed before Simone came bustling back to drop into her chair at the table. Evenou gave her a sharp glance, poured her some wine, watched her drink, then leaned closer across the table to ask a short question. Her reply was to produce the object she had just purchased in a shop in a neighbouring street. She placed it on the table.

The article she had left her lunch to purchase was a stout clasp-knife with a horn handle.

Evenou smiled, picked it up, hefted it against his palm, and put it down again. He nodded approval. Several persons at other tables saw the knife. When it was returned to Simone Deschamps' handbag the couple continued with their interrupted lunch.

Neither had lost an appetite.

When the meal was over they left the restaurant together. They went for a walk before turning into a café for some more drinks. Apparently details had to be agreed. Or maybe they had to find a suddenly flagging courage.

However that may be, when Simone Deschamps returned to her ground-floor apartment she was a ruthless woman without room in her mind for niggling doubt. She knew what she was going to do and was prepared to do it. The only bad patch was the waiting. Evenou had told her they must not be over-hasty. It had to be that night, but haste could spoil things. He had to prepare for the killer's visit.

Marie-Claire Evenou was also a good cook, and the gourmet who was over-partial to port wine found no satisfactory reason for denying himself the dinner his wife would have cooked. After all, it would be the last she would prepare for him.

But he found he could not face her across the dinner table, and took the easy way out. He gave her a barbiturate and talked quietly to her until she fell asleep. Then he tiptoed out of the room and, alone at the dining table, attacked the dinner prepared and cooked by the woman he had condemned to death sure in his knowledge that Simone Deschamps would not fail him.

Indeed, Yves Evenou's thoughts as he forked food into his lean mouth must have been of a curious quality. As a man of medical training he must have appreciated that in Simone Deschamps he was dealing with a woman who doubtless had a schizophrenic make-up. The seamstress who squinted for hours at needle and thread was one person. The ravenous sex-hungry lover was virtually a different person. Both inhabited the same body. Both obeyed him.

This obedience gave him the satisfactory sense of power that was as warming to his blood and as heady as the port wine that pleased his palate.

Over that lonely meal he felt like a Frankenstein about to test his ultimate control over a monster he felt was largely a creature of his own creation. After all, he had unleashed the evil in Simone Deschamps. He had taught her to revel in the obscene, he had helped her over five crazy years to acquire his own sense of being utterly without shame or remorse, to feel freed of normal inhibitions and to be ready at any time he ordered her to plunge into libidinous gratification of his own perverted desires.

As he sat back, listening to the ticking of the dining-room clock, it must have seemed that the short time remaining to his wife could be measured by her own heart-beats. He sat there obsessed by the thought of steel entering his wife's heart, and his concentration of mind made him restive for the time to pass more quickly.

He rose, went to his wife's side, stared at her passive face as he listened to her regular drugged breathing, then he looked at his watch, went out of the room, and collected his hat.

The flat seemed stifling.

There was still sunshine in the street outside, and heat rose from the pavements. He looked at his watch again, and decided he could go out for a breath of air. He could garage his car. It was an excuse.

He was out of the flat for half an hour, walking around the streets, trying, as it were, to grow sober. Not that he was drunk in any real alcoholic sense. But the culmination of his association with Simone Deschamps, as time for their fatal rendezvous approached, seemed to cloud his mind like wine fumes.

Or did his nerve fail, and did he have to take that walk to steel himself to go through with what he had planned?

Whatever the truth, when he returned to his flat at the end of that lonely half-hour spent in the streets that June evening he was ready to give the signal that would bring an armed murderess to his wife's door.

He picked up the telephone and dialled Simone Deschamps' number.

At the other end of the line Simone Deschamps sat in a chair awaiting the ringing tone. She was naked except for the high-heeled shoes on her feet and the black gloves covering her steady hands.

Her face was carefully made up. There was a glazed look about her large eyes.

Beside the telephone was the horn-handled knife.

At the first pealing ring she snatched the piece of black sensitized plastic from its cradle and held it to her ear.

'Now,' said a voice that always sent a strange tingling sensation through her, and had ever since the time of that first meeting when Yves Evenou had stared at her through his cigarette smoke in his consulting-room.

The line went dead. She replaced the receiver and, moving like someone in a dream state, reached for the overcoat she had ready. She shrugged into it, feeling its sleek lining cool against her warm nudity, and tugged it tight around her. She reached for the knife, slipped it in the coat's pocket, and turned to leave.

This was as arranged.

There was no hesitation on her part, no shrinking, and the steps she took towards the door did not stumble. In fact, after the door had snapped shut behind her she was able to run lightly up the flight of stone stairs to the Evenou apartment, her shoes tapping harshly until she reached the landing, where her heels beat a staccato tattoo to the door, which opened at once.

Evenou pulled her inside.

'No one saw you?'

She shook her head. 'No one.'

She took the knife from the coat's pocket, and he took the coat as she slipped out of it. Evenou pointed towards a door. He opened it, and they went into the room.

Marie-Claire Evenou, eyes closed, was in bed, breathing as she had before her husband took his after-dinner walk, more than half an hour before. Evenou gestured to one side of the bed.

Simone Deschamps sat down there, holding the glinting knife in her black-gloved hands, a fresh flush heightening the colour in her rather flat cheeks. Her mouth was pinched into a small bright knot of colour that was very like blood.

Evenou stooped over the other side of the bed and raised the bedclothes. He pulled them down, exposing his sleeping wife's body. He raised his right hand, folded the fingers until only the forefinger was outstretched, pointing.

'Look,' he said in a cold, matter-of-fact tone. 'There is the heart. Now strike there.'

He might have been giving a student a lecture in anatomy.

Obediently a black-gloved hand raised the knife it held, and the bright new blade intended to help make a camper's life easy flashed down to where the husband had pointed. But there was little force behind the blow. Simone Deschamps was willing. Her purpose was deadly. It was just that she lacked skill in murder. The blade drew blood, but the wound was little more than a savage scratch.

However, it was painful enough to awaken the wife, who cried out in fear.

'Yves—Yves——'

She stared aghast into her husband's smiling face, bent close over her.

'I'm here. You were having a nightmare.'

Well, it was truth of a kind. The nightmare was to continue relentlessly. Yves Evenou seized his appalled wife, and wrestled her struggling body into a prone position as he called to the naked woman to strike with her knife.

What followed was brutal butchery.

There was now great strength in Simone Deschamps' blows. Eleven times the knife slashed at the drugged and captive victim held by her husband. Horrible wounds were opened in her body. Steel mutilated her face.

Sixteen months later, in that crowded court-room of the Seine Assize Court, Judge Bonhoure asked the woman standing in the dock charged with murder, 'Why did you go that night to the Evenous' bedroom, naked except for your coat and wearing black gloves and red high-heeled shoes?'

The judge paused, leaned over his notes, and added in a cold clear voice, 'Was not this crime a climax to sexual perversion?'

The crowded court was silent for one dragging moment, then it was as though a collective shudder ran through it, as all eyes turned towards the woman, munching her lips before she replied to the Bench.

The judge spoke again, in the same severe voice.

'To go into all the details I have of your depravity I would have to clear this court. But why did you go upstairs naked? Was it to avoid bloodstains or in a sexual frenzy?'

The woman in the dock spoke.

'He ordered me to do it.' She munched her lips again, and appeared to shudder. 'I didn't want to, but I was afraid of him.

I loved him.' Her voice became stronger, rang through the court. 'He was everything to me, and I knew he would never agree to obtain a divorce.'

Judge Bonhoure was ready with the next point for clarification.

'After the stabbing,' he told her, 'the doctor went into the bathroom, but you sat there watching his wife's death agonies.'

Again her voice was lowered.

'I never meant to do it. I never thought I would,' she said. 'I hesitated because I did not want to, but he screamed: "You're just scared. Stab, stab!" I was afraid, and after that I do not know what happened.'

The whole sordid story was unfolded like a roll of stained bed-linen in the three days of the hearing. The all-male jury heard how Simone Deschamps had carefully cleaned the camper's knife after Marie-Claire Evenou had shuddered out her last breath. They frowned over the evidence of the demon lovers quarrelling after the pitiful remains of the wife had been seen by the police. First one of the accomplices had accused the other, then there had followed a counter-charge.

Yves Evenou, his health ruined by his excessive self-indulgence and dissipation, had died in prison while awaiting trial. His death left the woman who had wielded the camper's knife to stand alone in the dock.

But evidence had been obtained before Dr. Evenou collapsed and died of the incredible orgies of lust in which the demon lovers had indulged. Judge Bonhoure had the court cleared as he had intimated when this evidence was offered. In the judge's words the kind of sexual relations revealed in that evidence were 'beyond imagination'.

Such evidence made tantalizing and speculative reading, but it was not unhelpful to the defence's plea that Simone Deschamps was a woman 'bewitched' by her married lover. The sordid butchery was dressed up by the defence as a *crime passionnel.*

The jury sat impassively through the arguments, the claims, and the counter-claims. Judge Bonhoure was not quite so passive. His questions were penetrating and decisive in destroying the *crime passionnel* claim. The result of reconstruction of the crime, held by Paris detectives, left no one in doubt about the quality of the passion working in Simone Deschamps when she ran up the stairs in her red shoes, black gloves, and fur coat to kill a woman whose only injury to her had been her marriage to Yves Evenou years before.

Maître Fouquin demanded the guillotine for the woman in the dock.

Brushing aside, almost contemptuously, the claims of the defence, he insisted: 'She washed the bloodstained knife and gloves, and went to the trouble of sewing them into her mattress. That is not the attitude of a bewitched woman.'

But the counter-claims tried to undo the harm done by this picture of a woman whose actions had been deadly and remorseless. The defence strove to reveal another aspect of the woman in the dock, a woman with grey in her hair who had been normal until her meeting that day with Yves Evenou in his consulting-room. She had been destroyed by the evil in the man.

Simone Deschamps listened to both prosecutor and defending counsel with few signs that the arguments reached her. Occasionally she chewed her lip as she had when answering the judge's questions. But no tears welled in her eyes at the pitiful descriptions given by heated advocates. She remained dry-eyed throughout the entire three days. Even the demand for the guillotine did not make her flinch visibly. She seemed terribly resigned after giving her own direct answers.

But she did on one occasion voice regret for her terrible deed of blood. It was after the brother of the dead woman had given his evidence that she said in a choked voice: 'I am terribly sorry for what I did. I shall always feel the remorse.'

Those words saved her neck.

The charge was premeditated murder, and only extenuating circumstances could save her from the guillotine, and the jury had to find that there had been such extenuating circumstances.

'There are none,' the prosecutor declared roundly.

However, the jury in closed conclave remembered the words of regret, and decided that the woman who had uttered them might have been a woman of decent habits and honest affections before she met the man who unquestionably was her dark fate. They decided that, although she had committed a brutal murder, she had been dominated by the evil genius of the man who had died before he could stand beside her in the dock to share the awful weight of her crime.

They returned the verdict of guilty with extenuating circumstances.

Simone Deschamps remained dry-eyed when the verdict was proclaimed. Soberly she looked at Judge Bonhoure when he solemnly sentenced her to hard labour for life.

Her only sign of emotion was when her left hand stole to her right, on which she wore a small metal amulet.

The Paris reporters at the trial had referred to it as her good-luck piece or lucky charm.

The dry-eyed woman in the dock was superstitious and had carried her superstition into the place where she faced an ordeal that could conclude in an order for her death.

When she stepped from the dock, flanked by guards, she took her superstition with her. It was likely to prove very chill solace in the years ahead, for she looked like a woman in whom the spirit had died, leaving only a dry shell capable of enduring pain and the bitterness of memory.

2 * Double for Murder

'She's a good-looking woman, Clark.'

The man addressed turned from the bar and stared in the direction in which his companion was glancing. He saw a slim, tall brunette who stood waving her fan idly as she stared through the tall windows into the darkness of the gardens. He saw that her skin was a rich coffee colour. So she was an Anglo-Indian, like himself.

She turned, and their glances met and held before she lifted her fan and moved away towards the ballroom where couples were dancing to the rather ponderous melody produced by a military band.

'Well, don't you think so?'

Lieutenant Clark put down his glass and smiled at the man who had addressed him.

'A damned good-looking woman,' he said. 'Who is she?'

'Her name's Augusta Fullam,' he was told. 'She's the memsahib of the Deputy Examiner in Military Accounts. Pity Fullam isn't a dancing man.'

'I am,' Clark smiled and moved away from the bar.

A few minutes later he was dancing with Mrs. Edward Fullam in his arms.

Another man joined the bar companion Clark had left.

'I see Clark's dancing with Gussie Fullam,' he said. 'A new conquest?'

'I shouldn't wonder. So that's what she calls herself—Gussie. Well, she'll have to dance a dainty step to avoid scandal. Clark's reputation with the women is as solid as an oak door, and Meerut's a small place.'

All of which was substantially true. On that summer night in 1909, when Lieutenant Clark met Augusta Fullam for the first time and danced with her, he was a man with a reputation most local matrons considered tarnished. He held a commission in the Indian Subordinate Medical Service and was married to a woman who was six years older, and had been a nurse at the time she met Clark. It was rumoured that the present Mrs. Clark, who was usually treated in very cavalier fashion by her younger husband, had helped him in his studies and had even coached him for his exams, which he had not passed with any outstanding success.

No one in the Anglo-Indian community believed the Clarks to be happily married. There had been no romance and there existed no evidence of tenderness. Clark had wanted a commission in the Indian Subordinate Medical Service, which had opened its doors to Anglo-Indians as well as Europeans, and the nurse who was six years older had proved a necessary helper, standing by him when drunk, remaining when he became abusive and violent, and apparently the price of her constancy had been marriage. It had been a marriage of little more than convenience.

And apparently, according to the knowledgable in Meerut, what was sauce for the gander was equally sauce for the goose. If Clark went his own post-marital way, having a succession of wild affairs with other women, Mrs. Clark apparently reserved the right to find her own pleasures.

But whereas she was discreet, the same could not be said of her husband.

He revelled in his reputation as a ladies' man. As a medical man Lieutenant Henry Lovell William Clark was a very indifferent officer. He seemed more adept at making a career of women and wine.

He was well along in that career when he met Augusta Fairfield Fullam at the regimental dance. But whereas the wife of a respected Indian Civil Servant might have been expected to be repelled by the whisky-laden breath and possessive hands of a noted philanderer, the reverse was the case. She was not only attracted by this man who had sought her out, she was prepared to listen attentively to the suggestions he poured into the ear under her carefully arranged coiffure. They were not the kind of suggestions any gentleman was supposed to make to any lady upon such casual acquaintance.

But then Lieutenant Henry Clark, I.S.M.S., was no gentleman, despite the fact that he was an officer. Events were to prove that Gussie Fullam was no lady, although on that night of their first meeting in Meerut she certainly looked one.

However, in Meerut, as in most other places, appearances could be dreadfully deceiving.

One of the deceived was Edward Fullam.

He was a very reserved man, considered shy by a number of people, who preferred staying at home to enjoying the somewhat sluggish whirl of social activity in the Indian township. He liked his books and was in no sense a man's man. Club stories did not appeal to him, and he could no more become involved in an extra-marital liaison than he could become a party to doctoring the accounts it was his duty to examine and pass as authenticated and correct.

It was not difficult, as a matter of fact, to deceive a husband like Edward Fullam. He did not look for infidelity in his wife, and usually what he did not look for he did not see. Which is a purblind but rather comfortable way of blinking at reality until the scales are stripped from one's gaze.

Possibly, because of this, Augusta Fullam was a woman who was secretly feeling cheated by life at the time she met Clark. She had a daughter, but the girl doted on her father. She had a husband who was wrapped up in his career and his own affairs. The succeeding days assumed a dull complexion for her.

Then she listened to Clark's bold suggestions, felt the strength in his possessive hands, and suddenly the sun shone. It was as simple as that. This man with the bloated look, and the sensuous mouth half concealed by a trimmed military moustache, had the power to awaken something in her that became clamorous.

They were both Anglo-Indians. They shared the limitations of mixed blood in a European-dominated society. They wanted excitement. It was not a far step to obtain it—in each other's company.

Unquestionably each felt the tug of a strong animal attraction when they were together. If the woman had been what she wasn't she might have turned back from a liaison that could end only disastrously. But she had neither the will nor the wish to deny this man whose latent brutishness was a quality that curiously appealed to her.

So rather than drifting into a sordid affair, this strange couple rushed into one, clamorously, eagerly, each with a feeling that life was no longer defeating them. They arranged secret meetings. They conspired to have long hours together. They became lovers and indulged their shared desire to the full, until the physical attraction that was mutual became for a time the prime reason for shaping their lives.

When apart they wrote letters laden with excessive endearments and promises of further delights upon their next meeting.

It went on for more than a year. Possibly to the surprise of Harry Clark, who was undergoing the fresh experience of finding his brittle affections secured to one woman. For Augusta Fullam that year was no more than a natural time of emotional development that had been delayed by her marriage to an undemanding husband. She became the chattel of her dear Harry just as he became the doting lover of his lovely Gussie. Each enslaved the other. Both enjoyed a physical attraction that flamed passionately. Both mistakenly referred to what they shared as love.

Some weeks before Christmas in 1910 Harry Clark received orders posting him to Delhi. When told, the woman burst into tears of anguish. The prospect of being parted from this sensual lover whose attentions she craved filled her with panic.

On the last day of November she wrote him a most indiscreet and most passionate letter. With a florid romantic flourish she began it, 'Dear Heart of Mine', and continued with a banal greeting-card couplet:

'I greet you with loving thoughts and true,
And pray that every happiness may be vouchsafed to you.'

After pages of protestations and promises she concluded with 'Warmest love and sweetest kisses from your own little loving and ever devoted little sweetheart and Bucha—Gussie.'

Harry Clark was possibly touched by this avowal, and probably reassured, for he had no wish to break off the liaison that had been so gratifying in every way to a man of his coarse nature. He must have smiled at the use of the Hindu word for 'baby'. It had a lover's connotation almost a decade in advance of a similar usage by the writers of Tin Pan Alley after the close of the First World War.

His devoted little *bucha* was a rather matured thirty-six, and, as he had good reason to know, was pregnant.

It is curious that in a situation where most men of his philandering type might have considered themselves fortunate to be extricated by duty from what could become a social mess Harry Clark deemed himself ill-used by Fate. He told his little *bucha* as much in his follow-up letter. He was off to Delhi, but there was no question of old ties being snapped. Before he left Meerut he promised they would be together again.

It was one of the few promises he kept.

Again it was the working of the Indian Subordinate Medical Service that conspired to make this possible. Harry Clark had not been long in Delhi before he was given a fresh posting. This time to Agra. He was to take up a post in the Agra Station Hospital.

He arrived in the town famous for the proximity of the Taj Mahal to find some letters awaiting him. They were in his little *bucha*'s familiar handwriting. If Mrs. Clark cynically observed the letters lying around before her husband had collected them she was too wise to make comment. Letters in strange women's handwriting were no novelty in her life, especially when addressed to her husband. His succession of infidelities, his bouts of drunken indulgence—she had learned to live with them. She considered she had come to terms with life. She refused to act like a jealous wife. Maybe because it would have been acting. She was not jealous of her husband. All feeling for him on her part had died. She did not even hate him. In a sense she was free of him. Which made her free of his mistress of the moment.

One of the letters Clark read as soon as he had moved into his new bungalow in Agra insisted that his little *bucha* must see him without delay. 'I must, I must', wrote Augusta Fullam.

Clark was nothing loathe to arrange a meeting. It was on the 20th of April he took a train back to Meerut and met Gussie at a secret rendezvous. It was a wild reunion, with all the old heat of passion and the tug of that strange magnetism each exercised for the other.

'We've got to do something so we can be together. We can't go on like this,' the woman said softly, with her lips against her lover's ear.

Doing anything other than the routine of secret rendezvous and snatched moments quickly came to mean doing something about Edward Fullam. For once Clark found himself being urged to action by his mistress. He could have admitted the danger signal and left her had he not been so enslaved by her readiness to satisfy his desires.

She, on the other hand, would not have persisted in her exhortations if she had not found her husband, by contrast, an incubus and a burden she almost could not tolerate. Emotionally she was becoming too finely strung out. Something would snap under the pressure of her demands and desires.

Clark for his part, ignoring the danger, thought he could continue without doing anything drastic. He did not know what brooding in confinement in the Fullam home did to his little *bucha*. It made her introspectively savage. It made her brutal beyond her own nature.

She began to scare Clark. She told him her husband was showing signs of growing suspicious.

'If only he was not here everything would be simple,' she insisted.

It wasn't a great distance from that point to the consideration of murder. Once the ugly word was admitted, the means almost suggested themselves. Clark had a post in a hospital. He could come by poison with no great difficulty and little danger of being discovered.

So he returned to Agra and sent his mistress some powders containing arsenic.

She told Edward Fullam, who had been complaining of not feeling well, that she had bought him some recommended 'tonic powders'. He took them without any startling after-effects. Perhaps Clark had, in a moment of apprehension, played safe. But the wife became clamorous for a further supply, and the anxious lover in Agra procured some more powders, which he dispatched. As a matter of fact, enough of these 'tonic powders' were sent to ensure that, between April and July, Gussie could feed her husband a steady quantity of arsenic. It is understandable that, in the circumstances, Mrs. Fullam did not pay a great deal of attention to the running of her home. She certainly saw her husband's doctor when he called, but he admitted himself puzzled by the patient's continuing condition. In her moments of quiet she wrote letters to Agra. Some of them are very revealing, like this one:

> 'Oh, my darling, it seems too much to hope that before long the last barrier that separates us will be removed and you will be mine and I will be yours till the last.
>
> The thought is ecstasy; but at times my heart is full of fears. What if we fail! It would be too cruel! We must succeed. And what if we are discovered? This is too horrible a thought; and yet it often comes to me like a nightmare. God surely will not allow us to fail. He would not keep us apart, since we love each other so truly.'

The writer of that letter could have been teetering on the brink of an emotional abyss. But there is nothing in it to suggest that she was irrational to the point of being insane—except to be rid of her husband. Regularly dodging the doctor's puzzled questions with a show of wifely perplexity and feminine helplessness, she continued in secret poisoning her husband, feeling at the time no tiny encroachment of remorse, not even a flutter of guilt. She was a poisoner with a purpose, and that purpose was contained in the person of Harry Clark.

She was not a strong-willed woman. Indeed, rather otherwise. Like a good many Eurasians of the kind peopling the novels of Alice Perrin, she had a romantic streak that was as tough as forged steel. She could not forsake her well-nigh childish belief in romance for its own passionate sake. She did not see herself as a somewhat over-sexed woman seeking the one way to gratification she had found open to her. She convinced herself that what she and Clark had manufactured for each other was a grand passion. It was certainly more stimulating than the same commodity read about in a novel fresh out from England.

By the time the malignant summer was burning itself out, Edward Fullam was fighting a losing battle against the accumulation of arsenic in his system. His bewildered doctor sought out

Mrs. Fullam and said: 'I'm afraid your husband must go to hospital. He needs careful nursing. He is not responding as he should, and I am very worried.'

The sick man's wife raised no objection. As a matter of fact, she was very ready to fall in with the doctor's suggestion. She too agreed that her husband might be better off with professional nursing in hospital. She considered the Agra Station Hospital might offer the best solution. On this point the Fullams' doctor had no objection. Augusta Fullam was a persuasive woman when she smiled with a look of fluttering helplessness.

And her affair with Harry Clark had done nothing to impair her acknowledged good looks.

Accordingly arrangements were made for a transfer to Agra, and on the 8th of October the sick husband, accompanied by his attentive wife, arrived at the hospital where Harry Clark held an official appointment. He also held a letter received from his mistress shortly before the Fullams began their journey. It was a letter reflecting a new anxiety on the part of the woman who had been dosing her husband with Clark's arsenic.

In it she told him:

> 'Things are not going as they should. My hubby keeps the same—not a bit worse; and I fear we shall fail. Oh, God, give me strength to bear this bitter and cruel blow, and the disappointment and parting after all I have done and suffered. It isn't my fault, Harry darling. I have done all I could—all you told me. It is simply Fate.'

Gussie, his little *bucha*, was developing a neurosis that could become dangerous. Harry Clark, who had previously ignored danger signals, now recognized a new one. If she broke down under the self-induced mental strain the result could be catastrophic to his career, and his mixed blood demanded that he take any measure to retain the position he had so arduously attained with his wife's help. He had professional status. That he could not afford to lose.

He also had Gussie, whom he refused to give up.

The solution was simple. It was possibly too simple. Edward Fullam would be in the hospital where he had easy access to

C

poison cabinets and patients' rooms. He himself must take over the poison-giving from Gussie.

The solution also seemed logical to a harassed and groping mind. Besides, Clark already considered himself committed. If he had any doubt he had only to read his little *bucha*'s letters. He was already in over his ears, and that was very deep indeed.

When Edward Fullam arrived at the Agra hospital and was accommodated in a private ward Harry Clark realized he had one important detail in his favour as a murderer out to make up for lost time. The sick man had been ailing for months and, according to his case history, growing significantly weaker. His death would not provide any shock.

To the patient, Harry Clark was merely another commissioned Army doctor. Edward Fullam's attitude towards him was quite impersonal. The patient's spirits were very low on the evening of the 9th, when his daughter called to see him. Fullam had been one day in the hospital. Clark was in the room when the daughter sat by her father's bed. He must have heard the patient say the words that shocked the girl.

'I am going to die. I have a feeling that nothing can save me.'

The daughter burst into tears. She was till crying when Clark came forward with a hypodermic syringe in his hand and filled it from a wineglass on the table beside the patient's bed. Or so it appeared to her. He gave the patient an injection.

Suddenly the girl rose and ran from the sickroom, quite overcome.

Her father died the next day, the 10th. He was buried the following day, the 11th.

The new widow returned to Meerut to attend to her late husband's estate and to make arrangements for permanently transferring the family to Agra. It seemed a truly touching gesture, coming to live in the city where her husband had died. The time taken to wind up Edward Fullam's estate dragged for Harry Clark. He spent most of his free hours with a bottle. When he re-read Gussie's letters he found one that he pondered over. It was one of her more ebullient efforts, in which she wrote:

> 'The happy climax is coming, I think. Let us hope and pray that it will come soon, and that it will terminate in our happy

union and a long married life together, my best-beloved! I shall almost die of joy when it does come!'

Harry Clark's drink-fuddled memory was jogged savagely and he saw with sharp clarity precisely where he stood. Gussie wanted marriage. One obstacle, her husband, had been removed. A second remained. Clark's wife.

Harry Clark took to drinking more heavily, and even when the late Edward Fullam's widow was installed in her new home in Agra the whisky bottle remained his companion for far too long periods. But Gussie exerted her charm, and her animal high spirits when they were alone were infectious. Indeed, within mere weeks of Edward Fullam's death his widow appeared to have recovered remarkably from the tragedy.

She was seen frequently with Clark, now the good friend who had attended her poor husband, but when the pair were beyond prying eyes she evinced a startling new quality—jealousy. She wanted to supplant Mrs. Clark. She began upbraiding Clark when they were alone, and compensating for her behaviour by writing him more letters full of endearments and extravagant promises of delight. However, she usually closed with a coy warning about the wisdom of destroying her epistolary efforts.

Far from reading the warning and acting on it, Clark tied her letters in bundles and kept them in a metal box. He received a veritable spate of them. He tied them in bundles of fifty. Sometimes they came two or three times a day. Gussie, his little *bucha*, apparently had to fill her time in somehow. She had no husband to look after, and there is evidence that she did not suffer from writer's cramp, for by November of the next year, 1912, Clark had some four hundred of her letters in his black metal box. Edward Fullam had been dead a little over a year.

So far as Gussie the prolific letter-writer knew, none of her literary indiscretions existed.

Gradually she adopted a more insistent attitude, and Clark came to the point where drinking no longer helped. Only action would appease her, and he brooded over the best way to rid himself of his wife.

Poison was out. This time he not only wanted nothing to do with actual participation in a crime. He wanted clean hands and an alibi. It seemed there was only one practical solution. If thieves broke into the bungalow and killed his wife no finger could point to Harry Clark.

His Hindu cook was a man of many curious contacts in the bazaars. For years past he had proved helpful when Harry Clark sought the kind of company usually kept behind locked doors and curtained windows. He now agreed, for a consideration, to make contact with a leader of *badmashes*. Being a man of his word, he soon notified his master that a visit could be expected from a very discreet stranger, prepared to talk terms for a special service to the sahib.

The furtive stranger told Clark he always worked with three assistants, and all of them would demand to see their employer to receive payment. A little later Clark met the four Hindus who were prepared to commit murder for a fixed price per head. Apparently each had to give the cook, a rather business-like character, a separate rake-off. In return the cook would be available to open the door of the bungalow on the following Sunday evening.

That Sunday was the 17th of November. Clark had carefully arranged to be invited out for the night. Before he left to establish his alibi he called on Augusta Fullam, bearing a locked black metal box, and asked her to mind it for a few days.

'It holds some personal papers I don't wish to leave in the bungalow while I'm away,' he told her.

Little did his little *bucha* realize as she took the box from him that she was receiving back every letter she had written him, on a number of which she had even written: 'Destroy this without delay.'

She put the box in a cupboard and gave it no further thought. After all, she had plenty to think about that week-end. The *badmashes* had been paid. Before the week-end was over Harry Clark would have no wife. A short period of mourning, for the sake of appearances and propriety, and then she would become Mrs. Henry Lovell William Clark, and her life would have been changed completely round the way she wanted it. Her dream would have become reality. She did not dwell on the two acts of murder that would have made this possible.

But it was one of the longest week-ends she had lived.

While Harry Clark was away from home that Sunday night the

four thugs crept through the bungalow garden, gave the agreed signal on the door, and were let in by the waiting cook. One of them carried a lantern. By its light they beat Mrs. Clark to death.

Harry Clark and Augusta Fullam met outside the city. Both were excited as they kissed within a short distance of the fabulous Taj Mahal. Their excitement would have withered if they had realized they were meeting as lovers for the last time.

By the time they had returned to Agra a determinedly efficient Inspector Smith of the local police was making inquiries about the bungalow murder, and had already caught a very nervous cook telling a lie. Inspector Smith did not take long deciding he might not be wasting his time if he called on Lieutenant Clark's friend, Mrs. Fullam.

What should have been a routine visit apparently unnerved the widow. She virtually collapsed when Inspector Smith began asking questions. He decided he should search her home, and he came across the locked black metal box. When he learned it was Clark's, he had it opened, and was surprised at the collection of letters tied in fifties. There were more than four hundred in all, and the methodical recipient had noted the date of receipt on the envelope of each and appended his initials.

Inspector Smith arrested the Clark cook, who promptly confessed, and the murderous lovers. He asked Mrs. Fullam's daughter to make a formal statement about her visit to her father a few hours before his death. In that statement she said:

> 'Lieutenant Clark was in the room at the time, and I saw him dip a needle into a wineglass and inject something into my father. After I had gone to bed I heard some strange gurgling noises from the room, which alarmed me, but they soon ceased, and I fell asleep, worn out with crying. The next morning I was told that my father was dead.'

The scandal of a double murder burst like a bombshell in Agra. When the details became known and the letters quoted the English community was rocked. It was learned that Clark had offered from his cell to marry the woman who had shared his crime, and who was again pregnant with a child of his.

'No!' she cried at the police emissary. 'Nothing would induce me to marry him. He is the cause of all my trouble. But for him I should be a free and happy woman today. He has poisoned and wrecked my life.'

Gone were the lavish sentiments and endearments of the four hundred impulsive letters. Augusta Fairfield Fullam had come right through her false romanticism and stood appalled at the reality confronting her. She had no mercy now that passion had smouldered to cold ash.

For Clark it can at least be said he tried to act like the gentleman he had never succeeded in being during his days as an officer. He took the complete blame for the double murders on himself, trying desperately to exonerate the woman. In a lengthy and carefully considered statement he wrote of Edward Fullam's murder:

> 'I had no wish or intention to kill him. My only wish was to get him out of the way, to make him so ill that he would be obliged to leave India, and thus leave the field clear for me.'

A little naive, surely. A husband could be expected to take his wife with him. However, he continued more positively:

> 'But I found that I had gone too far. I saw at last that he was dying, that nothing could save him. When I gave him a final dose that finished him. And this, I swear, I did out of pity, just to put an end to his misery.'

At the trial both partners in the double murder were found guilty. Harry Clark was sentenced to death, the pregnant Augusta Fullam to life imprisonment. The officer who had not been a gentleman until too late was hanged on the 26th of March, 1913, before the birth of his illegitimate child, whose mother died in prison on the 29th of May, 1914.

3 * The Chocolate Killer

On a bright, sunny day in 1870 a woman who certainly did not look her age, and who was thought by her neighbours to be all of ten years younger than she in fact was, left a house in fashionable Gloucester Place, Brighton, to go for a walk along the front. She was most elegantly dressed in clothes that suited her tall, slim figure, and under her trim bonnet was fair hair that caught masculine glances.

It certainly caught the eye of a gentleman who passed her along the promenade. The woman looked up, met his approving stare, and was there and then reduced to a state of fluttering excitement that would have been more appropriate in a person half her age.

Something had happened in the brief time of those exchanged glances that filled Christiana Edmunds' life with wonder and was doomed later to fill it with tragedy.

She had fallen in love. Ironically, the glance of the passer-by had been completely impersonal. He had looked at the bright golden hair, not the face it framed, although that face held charm and the unmistakable evidence of good middle-class upbringing. The eyes in that face were bright and wide and in that day could have been termed without too much exaggeration lustrous. They certainly gave no hint that the mind to which Victorians believed they were the index was not perfectly balanced.

However, it was only as the poet's index that the eyes could be faulted. As organs of sight, for which nature intended them, they were well-nigh perfect. They were certainly at times quite breathtaking.

Possibly because Dr. Beard, a popular physician of the seaside resort, had not looked into the wide blue eyes that went with the arresting fair hair he had no suspicion of the effect his casual interest had made upon the lady in flowered grey silk. However, the lady herself was quickly determined to rectify the omission.

She found no difficulty in establishing the identity of the masculine charmer who had looked at her and caused her heart to skip a few beats. When she was assured he was a married medical man with a family she refused to be dismayed by the appalling marksmanship of Dan Cupid. For her to tell herself she was in love was to believe it.

After all, she had reached an age far beyond mere discretion. She was forty-two. She looked thirty-two, and allowed herself to admit she was thirty-three. So she was not unpractised at living on her own terms.

She also lived with her mother, the widow of an architect and an engineer who had spent most of his career in Margate, where he had left his mark by designing the lighthouse and some public edifices before his tragic death. The sorrowing widow had exchanged a seaside resort of sad memories for another with the promise of a bright future. By 1870 Christiana was her only surviving child. Which came to mean that the fair-haired daughter of over forty was often treated and petted like a child.

Certainly when Christiana took to her bed a day or so after her walk along Brighton front her mother showed every sign of being worried.

'I can't think what you've eaten, dear, that could cause you to feel so poorly,' wailed Mrs. Edmunds. 'I think I had better send for the doctor.'

'Do, Mama,' said Christiana, her eyes very wide, her hair a pale cloud on her pillow. 'Dr. Beard. I've heard such wonderful reports about him.'

'I've never heard of Dr. Beard,' the mother protested.

'I've got his address in my little notebook, dear Mama.'

It was not long after this exchange that Dr. Beard arrived at the house in Gloucester Place opposite the church of St. Peter's. The comely physician who was ignorant of how he had made his patient's heart flutter might have been surprised at how rapidly she progressed under his treatment, considering he had found very little wrong with her, but he was left in no doubt that she was a lovely woman who enjoyed his company, and he felt flattered. The mixture of flattery and charm can be a heady one. It was so in Gloucester Place. Dr. Beard was forcibly reminded, by the evidence of his own eyes, that he was a man. That should have given him pause. It didn't. It encouraged him to allow a friendship to ripen. Naturally a flattering friendship.

To be quite fair, the doctor might have found his new patient attractive and interesting, and he could have considered her charming and delightful without being in the slightest degree aware that the lady felt about him in any less-detached way.

But he was a fool to agree to her writing to him in the lavish style she promptly adopted. And if he wasn't, then he should have terminated the correspondence abruptly, even brutally, after receiving the first letter addressed to 'Caro Mio', in which there was a reference to 'long kisses'. The writer signed herself 'Dorothea'.

Dr. Beard might have been in a quandary at finding he had allowed something to start he might not be able to close without losing a valuable patient. For Gloucester Place certainly suggested money. Anyway, he adopted what proved a tragic alternative to a little firm verbal surgery. He introduced Miss Edmunds to his wife. Professional interest became merged with social. The fair-haired woman who believed herself in love with another woman's husband soon became a friend of the Beard family.

That did not stop the flow of letters to 'Caro Mio' from 'Dorothea'. They continued, couched in such terms that should have produced a few furrows in the manly brow of the handsome husband and father. Not a bit of it. Dr. Beard was becoming used to another woman's flattery. He enjoyed it. He kept the letters and read them over again at his leisure. Far from alarming him by their very protestations, they gave him an enjoyment he did not feel compelled to share with his wife. Indeed, he neither showed her the letters nor told her he had received them.

They became a secret shared between the handsome doctor and his good-looking patient, who had become a friend of the family. By the time 'Dorothea' was referring to 'la Sposa', as she invariably described Mrs. Beard in her correspondence with the man she loved, in terms of downright contempt it was, of course, too late to think of letting the wife into the secret. Especially as 'Dorothea' was hinting, and rather broadly, that she would like to be on more possessive terms with 'Caro Mio'.

Perhaps the time had gone by when Dr. Beard could have ended it all without some sort of fuss or even a domestic explosion. But by continuing to do nothing except read the letters and store them away for possible future reference—otherwise why store them?—he did nothing to bring the curious relationship to an end.

In fact, he encouraged its continuance, for Christiana Edmunds, the friend of the Beard family, still called at their home and brought occasional gifts for 'la Sposa'. One such gift, in March, 1871, was a box of chocolates.

On this occasion the family's fair-haired friend arrived in the afternoon, when Mrs. Beard was alone.

'This is an unexpected pleasure,' the doctor's wife, invariably the polite hostess, welcomed the unexpected guest. 'I'm afraid I'm on my own.'

'Lovely. We can have a pleasant chat.'

From the exchanges an onlooker would never have guessed Christiana Edmunds was talking to 'la Sposa' of the letters from 'Dorothea'.

The two women went into the drawing-room, and after some desultory but easy conversation about topics of the day the visitor unwrapped the box of chocolates.

'I brought you these, my dear Mrs. Beard, because I am so fond of them myself. Now just taste the flavour of this chocolate cream.'

Christiana Edmunds chose a large chocolate from the unbroken rows of the top layer, and, standing up and leaning towards the other woman, pushed it into her mouth. Mrs. Beard, rather surprised at this forceful insistence, had no recourse but to open her mouth, receive the chocolate behind her teeth, and start munching.

Almost immediately a look of knotted distaste crossed her features.

'Oh,' she gasped, 'it's quite horrible. I can't swallow it. Something must have gone bad in it.'

She lifted her handkerchief and removed the nauseating chocolate mess from her mouth.

'I've never known this to happen before,' said the wide-eyed visitor. 'Here, try another. To take the taste out of your mouth.'

She quickly chose a chocolate from a different row and advanced on the seated woman, who threw up her hands.

'No, I couldn't, Miss Edmunds,' she protested. 'I'm afraid I swallowed a little of that other chocolate, and it's made me feel quite sick.'

'Has it?' asked Miss Edmunds brightly.

Shortly afterwards she took her leave. She seemed not at all concerned by the unusual *contretemps*. That may have been because she had taken the precaution of not leaving the remainder of the box of chocolate creams.

However, some hours later Mrs. Beard was reminded of the visit when she experienced a sharp stomach pain and a feeling of nausea that made her head swim. She said nothing to her husband of the visit when he returned home from his calls, but she felt she had reason to mistrust Miss Edmunds and her chocolates. For two days she kept her misgivings to herself, but she had been a doctor's wife sufficiently long to know some of the symptoms of poisoning, and she now believed her visitor had tried to poison her, no less.

She told her husband. At first he ridiculed such a notion, but when his wife detailed the pains she had felt, and the accompanying nausea, he frowned, thoroughly perturbed.

'Leave this to me, my dear,' he said. 'I'll deal with that young lady. She won't step foot inside this house again, never fear.'

Now that it was almost too late he shook himself out of his indulgent lethargy and sent word to Gloucester Place that he wished to see Miss Edmunds upon a very personal and confidential matter.

The two met, and this time it was no meeting of 'Dorothea' with her 'Caro Mio'. A thoroughly indignant and outraged husband and father told Christiana Edmunds of his wife's accusation.

'Furthermore,' he said, before she could interrupt or protest her innocence, 'I'm inclined to believe it is the truth, that you did try to poison her, and I must tell you that you will no longer be welcome at my home, nor do I wish you to call upon my services in any professional capacity.'

'Dorothea' was for once without ready words at her command, although her eyes snapped angrily. 'Caro Mio', having said his piece, beat a hasty and very tactical retreat, for Dr. Beard had seen the beginnings of an emotional storm blowing up over an horizon much closer than the one across the Channel.

Christiana Edmunds hurried home. When she arrived she was beside herself and behaving like a woman whose control had snapped abruptly.

'The doctor has charged me with attempting to murder his wife!' she cried to an amazed and badly shaken Mrs. Edmunds. 'Me! Murder! I shall go mad!' She flung her arms about and looked thoroughly distrait. 'I shall go mad! Oh, I shall go mad!'

Mrs. Edmunds looked at her through eyes filled with tears. There was a terrible truth alive and demanding in the mother's tired brain, one she had kept to herself for years, hoping that it would never be made manifest.

Now that hope had died swiftly.

She said, her voice choking, 'My poor child, you are mad already!'

This announcement, uttered in a broken voice, brought sudden stillness to the younger woman. Her arms dropped. She looked at her mother, shocked, realizing that the words were meant.

It was for mother and daughter a frightening moment of truth. Mrs. Edmunds broke the unnatural quiet by sharing her long-kept family secret. There was a history of violent insanity on both sides of the family. But before the announcement was completed a new look of wild intensity was blazing in the daughter's large eyes.

'He must withdraw it!' she shouted. 'There must be an apology. I will have an apology.'

The moment of stark truth was shattered, lost. The daughter behaved like a wild woman, insisting over her mother's objections and counsel of caution that she would demand an apology from the man who had bitterly maligned and insulted her.

When her mother said it would be wiser to forget the incident she cried: 'I will have my name cleared. I will! I will!'

Mrs. Edmunds nodded, dried her eyes, and helped compose the very formal letter to Dr. Beard, in which he was warned that unless his recent slander on her daughter was withdrawn without delay proceedings would be taken against him in the courts.

The letter was posted. It brought no reply, much less a withdrawal of the charge.

Dr. Beard, the letters from 'Dorothea' locked away from prying eyes, sheltered behind a wall of dignified silence. Undoubtedly relations between husband and wife in the Beard home were strained. Mrs. Beard was an intelligent woman and quite able to come to the right conclusion when she considered assorted facts. But she had won her personal battle. Any demonstration from her side might lose the moral advantage she had obtained. So the continued silence was condoned.

However, in Gloucester Place it was construed by an anguished 'Dorothea' as further insult, because she was now under the compulsion to prove her innocence to 'Caro Mio', still, despite her bitterness and wailing, the sole object of her ingrown affection. When she no longer acted like a woman deranged she fell to contemplating the possible ways open to her for securing redress. She saw herself as someone who had failed in a first attempt. But she could try again. More subtly, with greater skill. This time she would succeed.

Her contempt for 'la Sposa' had turned to a sour hate.

And Christiana Edmunds had become determinedly deadly. She could translate her new resolve into action more stimulating than writing letters with a tendency to repetitious phrasing. She had found small occasion in the sheltered years of her past to employ a cunning which she hardly realized she possessed. But now she discovered she could be truly devious, and the discovery was exciting.

As far as the troubled mother was concerned, her daughter had recovered from a tantrum that might even have been a delusion. Mrs. Edmunds wanted only silence and prayed that the postman would bring no letter to destroy the uneasy calm pervading her home.

She watched her daughter go for her lonely walks along the front, and hoped that the invigorating sea air would help to restore her lost inner calm. Mrs. Edmunds, who had confided her grim secret in a moment when she was sorely troubled, had no fear for her own sanity, and those she had entertained about her daughter seemed to be largely unjustified as days passed with Christiana returning to the fusty but friendly routine that life had become in the large house before she went for that walk when a stranger had glanced at her.

However, this time it was the daughter who had a secret she was keeping to herself. She gave a watchful mother no hint of what she was planning.

On one of her afternoon walks she turned from the front towards one of the poorer parts of the town, where some children were playing in the street. She beckoned to a boy, and when he approached asked him if he would run an errand for her. Ready to earn a few coppers, the boy agreed.

'Very well,' she said, giving him a bright smile. 'I want you to go to a certain shop and buy some chocolate creams. I shall be waiting at the corner of Portland Street, where you are to bring them. Now can you do that?'

'Yes, lady.'

'You won't run away with the chocolate creams?'

'No, lady.'

'Good. Now listen very carefully.'

She told him the name of the shop, what to buy, and precisely where to meet her. Then she gave him the exact money, making sure that he would not be tempted to run away with any change.

When the boy with the bag of chocolate creams arrived at the street corner where the unknown lady had said she would be his face lit up. She was there, as she had said she would be. She took the bag of chocolates from him and gave him some coppers, and he darted away. Christiana Edmunds smiled after him, reflecting that it had been very simple so far. She felt elated on her walk back to Gloucester Place.

In the seclusion of her room she produced the remains of the strychnine she had obtained for poisoning the box of chocolates. It is reasonable to suppose that Christiana Edmunds was in no way ungenerous with the amount of poison she inserted into the sweetmeats. When she had treated each chocolate and sealed it she returned the deadly confections to the paper bag supplied by the shop.

A day or so later she took the bag of poisoned chocolates out with her, concealed in her muff, when she started for her afternoon walk. She followed the earlier routine. Walking into a poorer part of the town, she found another boy who was ready to take the chocolates back to the shop where they had been purchased with the request that the confectioner change them because the lady had wanted the smaller English chocolate creams, not the larger French ones.

The shopkeeper proved readily obliging. He tipped the large chocolate creams into the box from which they had been taken and weighed up a similar quantity of the smaller variety. The boy took the fresh chocolates back to where the lady was waiting for them, received some pennies for having made the errand, and went on his way rejoicing. She repeated this manœuvre on several subsequent occasions.

Christiana Edmunds was now a dealer in death, although that did not concern her. She was concentrating on what she hoped the effect of her conniving would be on 'Caro Mio'. Someone would purchase poisoned chocolates from the shop. There would be an outcry, and she could demonstrate to Dr. Beard that she was in no way responsible for the bad sweetmeat his wife had tasted.

This too seemed simple and uncomplicated when she surveyed it.

She did not have to wait long for a noisy reaction to her cunning.

Little Sidney Albert Barker, who was four, took a chocolate from a bag of sweets his uncle had bought and ate it ravenously. He could hardly have tasted it or he would have spat it out. Twenty minutes later he was dead.

The doctor who examined the child reported the death to the local coroner. At the inquest several people came forward to claim they had been ill after tasting some horrible chocolates purchased at the shop which sold the poisoned sweets to little Sidney's uncle. The coroner adjourned the inquest, and the police called at the shop which sold chocolate creams of at least two kinds. A distressed shopkeeper told them he had burned his entire stock of such sweetmeats.

At the resumed inquiry a lady unknown to the Barker family and to the coroner came forward to give evidence. She said she had known of unpleasant chocolates being sold by the same shop and of friends who had been made ill by them. She even claimed that on one occasion after she herself had eaten one of the chocolates she had become 'ill and dizzy, and had a burning sensation in my throat'. She told the coroner she had complained to the shopkeeper, but he had told her with some indignation that he had never had such a complaint before and that he bought his stock only from firms of really sound reputation.

Following this spirited piece of evidence was that of Dr. Lethaby, who had attended the dead boy. He said the child had died of strychnine poisoning.

However, after the coroner's jury had returned the not very satisfactory verdict of 'Accidental death' it was not Dr. Lethaby whose name was on the tongues of most people in Brighton but Christiana Edmunds, the woman who had come forward to help the inquiry.

The local newspapers, as well as most of the nationals, reported the case, and it must be concluded that Dr. Beard, the reason for the enactment of the entire tragic farce, read of this underlined vindication of a 'Dorothea' who belonged to some weeks before yesterday.

But no word from him was received at the house in Gloucester Place, where Christiana Edmunds waited in her room, her active mind following the train of a fresh development that appealed to her.

She would have that apology she had demanded. She would make 'Caro Mio' see how wrong he had been to blame 'Dorothea'. To achieve that, and to savour the sweetness of achievement, became an obsession.

Letters from an unknown using such aliases as 'Seeker of Justice' and 'Indignant Tradesman' arrived at the home of the dead boy's father, urging him to bring an action against the unfortunate shopkeeper who had sold the poisoned chocolates. Their receipt was reported in the local Press.

Shortly afterwards some Brighton residents received by post gift boxes of fruits, flowers, and cake, with a letter in a strange hand that betrayed intimate knowledge of the recipient. A number of those receiving such unexpected gifts became ill. One of the persons singled out for such a gift had the following note included in the package:

> 'A few home-made cakes for the children. Those done up are flavoured on purpose for yourself to enjoy. You will guess who this is from. I can't mystify you, I fear. I hope this arrives for you tonight while the eatables are fresh.'

A most curious missive.

The majority of the parcels were posted in Brighton, but some had been handed in at a London post office. Apparently Christiana Edmunds was remembered by the mysterious donor, for she went to the police, told them they were idiots, no less, and demanded that they act quickly and produce some results. Her demands were accepted by a stone-faced officer who recalled that this militant female was the woman who had received the publicity at the time of the Barker boy's inquest.

However, the militant Miss Edmunds did get some action. The town's Chief Constable had an advertisement inserted in the *Brighton Daily News* on August 17th, 1871, in which a reward of twenty pounds was offered for information that would lead to the arrest of the mysterious dispenser of poison.

Again Brighton felt a shock wave of apprehension. One reader of the Chief Constable's advertisement who experienced a more personal shock was a certain chemist who recalled supplying strychnine to Miss Christiana Edmunds. He made a point of informing George White, the Chief Constable, who lost no time in sending Inspector Gibbs to investigate this woman who had been so apparently public-spirited.

Gibbs examined a number of letters used by Christiana Edmunds to procure various quantities of strychnine. The signatures were found to be forgeries. Next the handwriting was compared with the letters received by Sidney Barker's father. Remarkable examples of similarity were discovered. The same was the case when comparison was made with a few of the notes included in the parcels of poisoned cakes and fruits.

After that it was not very long before the inspector called on Dr. Beard. When he left the doctor's house Gibbs had a very fair understanding of what had happened. When he told the Chief Constable the anxious George White was appalled at the extent of a determined woman's duplicity.

Christiana Edmunds was sitting in her room, possibly wondering when Dr. Beard would write his letter of grovelling apology, and undoubtedly feeling she had been ingenious, when her mother announced that a police inspector wanted to see her. Feeling that the police she had jogged into action had come to her for further assistance, and at the same time very assured that she could continue with her deadly masquerade, she went downstairs to be confronted by a grave-faced Gibbs, who told her, 'I arrest you on a charge of murdering Sidney Barker by administering poison to him.'

Two days after the police advertisement appeared in the local newspaper Christiana Edmunds appeared in the Town Hall police court before a group of frowning magistrates.

With adjournments, the inquiry went on for weeks. Crowds beseiged the court, and one reporter claimed that the numbers queuing for admission before the doors opened 'was a sight to break a theatre manager's heart with envy'.

Christiana Edmunds was giving Brighton one of its greatest free shows. Pen-and-ink sketches of her were on sale in the streets, but her only comment when she was shown one was that it did not do her justice. Which could have been a most truthful remark.

She was poised and calm throughout the lengthy hearing, and even when Dr. Beard in a faltering voice told of his association with her and produced 'Dorothea's' letters she gave no sign of emotional disturbance. She was apparently calling on unsuspected reserves that she was to need in the future. Almost overnight 'Dorothea' had been submerged in the woman who was charged with murder, and 'Caro Mio' had been, for her, relegated to her lost yesterdays. This monumental change in a woman who had conceived a deadly purpose and pursued it with undeviating resolve was sufficiently startling to make a few of the more perceptive students of her strange case consider the possibility of her mind being unbalanced.

She was committed for trial at Lewes winter assizes on the double charge of murdering Sidney Barker and of attempting to murder Mrs. Beard, but because of the strong feeling against her throughout Sussex she was eventually taken to London for trial at the Central Criminal Court.

Throughout the two days of that trial the Old Bailey court-room was packed, and there was a dramatic highlight that left everyone in court hushed and sober. That was when Mrs. Edmunds took the witness-stand to tell in a choked voice her own secret story of a family she described as 'saturated with lunacy'.

Standing there in black, unable to glance at her daughter in the dock, her voice faltering, she was the object of pity from all her hearers when she related how her husband had died in Earlswood Asylum at the age of forty-seven. Christiana's brother had died in another asylum, while her sister had tried to commit suicide by hurling herself from a window. She confessed that her own father had been insane during his last years and had died in an epileptic fit, while one of her nieces had suffered the same affliction.

The pathetic parade of family ghosts and skeletons came to an end with the sudden awful breakdown of the prisoner. Her calm gave way to a torrent of surcharged tears. But over-late tears could not wash away the terrible stain of guilt, and while the judge, Sir Samuel Martin, gave a fair summing-up, he had to point out to the jury that the prisoner had seemed well aware of what she was doing and understood the consequences of her deliberate acts. After a lengthy absence the jury found her guilty.

The recovered prisoner, when asked by the judge if she had anything to say, sprang back to her former self with a startling resiliency. Gone were the tears. Clear and ringing was her voice as she asseverated: 'It is owing to my having been Dr. Beard's patient that I have been brought into this position. I wish the jury could have known the exact particulars of his intimacy with me, and the way I have been treated.'

Whereupon she tried to give them an idea by claiming she was pregnant, but a panel of hard-eyed matrons, after examining her, informed the court that the claim was false.

Sir Samuel Martin donned the black cap and solemnly sentenced her to death.

The *Brighton Daily News* next day voiced sentiments that sound well-nigh barbarous a century later. Its leader proclaimed:

> 'Better that a dozen mad murderers should be hanged than that one sane murderer should escape, for, after all, what is death to an insane person? If, in spite of all our care, a really insane person should be put to death, there would be little reason to grieve for one who had been delivered from a world of illusions cruel to himself and dangerous to all around.'

In the capital the *Daily Telegraph* thundered in a vastly different key. It roundly declared:

'If this wretched, half-crazed creature, the sister, daughter, and grandchild of lunatics, is put out of the world in deference to a judicial definition of the plea of insanity, her death will bring disgrace upon British justice.'

While the country debated whether Christiana Edmunds should die, Sir Samuel Martin wrote a confidential letter to the Home Secretary. The outcome was that the sentence of death was commuted to detention during Her Majesty's pleasure. Christiana Edmunds was removed to Broadmoor, where she lived for more than thirty years. She died in 1907, convinced that she was a great lady being kept in confinement by powerful enemies because she knew their dire secrets.

Like the former 'Dorothea', the woman in Broadmoor was a letter-writer. There were times when she was convinced she was back in her own home, and then she wrote letters to many famous names, extending invitations to tea. The letters were never posted. Nor was she discouraged from writing them. Like 'Dorothea', the letter-writer in Broadmoor caused less trouble than the woman who put down her pen and began thinking of what else she could do—with deadly determination.

4 * The Shotgun Divorce

Among the myriad races that make up the United States of America few are as proud of their ancestral line as the Cajuns of Louisiana. Few are more ingrown.

The Cajuns have French-sounding names derived from the settlers who were granted licence by Louis the Fourteenth to make homes and to carve an empire out of the wilderness to the north of the Mississippi delta. In this land of cypress swamps and dark bayous fringed with curtains of Spanish moss the Cajuns settled and conquered the rich alluvial soil without thinning their blood by frequent marriage with folk they considered outlanders.

Indeed, they have fiercely preserved racial characteristics they have come to look upon as a heritage. Shrewd, hard-working, hard-living, essentially uncomplicated, they have maintained a curious integrity which today, in a nation where progress is a religion for materialists, is virtually an anachronism. Tough peasant sinews and equally tough peasant outlooks on life have not weakened noticeably in the changing centuries. However, restricted biology at times has produced some strange domestic upheavals among the Cajuns.

Few stranger than in the Lemoine family.

Louis Paul Lemoine was one of twelve children born to parents of Cajun stock. He grew up quiet and shy and retiring, afraid to mingle with strangers. It could hardly be otherwise. Louis was born a deaf mute.

He grew as a child to love the swamp-lands. As a youth he

became a good shot, and would vanish for days into the wilderness his ancestors had known. His family were not bothered. Louis could not speak to strangers, but then strangers could not hear his approach. Louis was as much at home in the forest glades of the Red River watershed as sitting at the family table for Sunday dinner.

He married late by Cajun standards. But by their standards he chose a wife much younger than himself. Addie Mae Lavespere was fifteen when she married the deaf mute. She married him to escape the drudgery of her home life and to have an opportunity of managing a home of her own. She had fair hair that fluffed out over her shoulders, dark thoughtful eyes that at times held a smouldering intensity, and her face was lean, with a firm chin-line.

Louis had left school in his early teens. The fact that he was backward at any kind of scholarship was accepted by all who knew him as natural enough. How he managed to declare his love for Addie Mae and ask her to marry him is one of the mysteries shared by the pair of Cajun lovers.

Louis Paul Lemoine was twenty-three when, with Addie Mae clinging to his arm, he stood before the preacher in Natchitoches, the little swamp town where Addie Mae was born, and made signs that he wanted this girl to be his wife and share his worldly goods, which were pitifully few.

The girl bride and the deaf mute husband left Natchitoches to set up home in the Clouterville area, where Louis could make a living as a logger. It was hard work and tiring physically. Louis tried working as a farmhand in between his spells of logging, which was seasonal work at best. Every dollar he earned came from labouring with earth in some way. He was no reader. He could hold no conversation with the few friends they made. He had his gun and his dog, and for relaxation he took to the woods he had known from boyhood.

Not surprisingly, it was a poor sort of marriage.

There were children for the bride wife to look after. Seven in all, and the first was born within a year of the newly-weds arriving in the Clouterville area. But offspring did not serve to unite parents who grew apart. Addie Mae, growing older, aware that other women went to parties, had noisy fun, came to resent a home almost stifled by the father's silence. By whatever means she had of communicating with the man she had married she told him she wanted to go out and be with friends, to sit among bright lights occasionally. Addie Mae was a Cajun, but she was also a woman with a woman's natural longings for escape from daily routine and for admiration from appreciative male glances. Yet she was no capricious flirt. She was a mother who did not spare herself in the upbringing of her children.

But by the time she was twenty-eight she had had enough of living as Louis's wife.

She informed him she was getting a divorce.

'I can't carry on,' was the tenor of her complaint to her ever-silent husband. 'I'm going to get a divorce and leave you.'

He looked at her, and continued looking.

'I mean it,' she insisted.

He picked up his gun and went out. She stood in the unpainted doorway and saw him walking towards the woods. He did not look back. It was three days later when he returned home. He was unshaved, there was dried blood on his clothes, and mud on the stock of his gun. He ate a meal, shaved and washed, and went to bed after cleaning his gun. Next morning he went back to work. There was no word about divorce.

But Addie Mae was a young woman whose mind, once made up, had a habit of staying that way.

She went to a lawyer. She produced her savings. She explained what she wanted.

In 1955 a court order granted her wish. She was Mrs. Lemoine in name only.

But she was still the mother of a growing brood. The divorced Mrs. Lemoine found that her new-won freedom had fetters she had not previously considered. Her children needed not only a mother. They needed a father. Even one that was deaf and dumb.

So the new divorcée found her way back to the little house behind the trees close to the white-rail fence bordering on the unpaved road. Louis looked at her when he opened the door, then stood back.

In the familiar living-room there was another strange discussion between the now legally separated parents. The very nuances and insistence that must have been inherent in their wordless debate could only have been guessed. Yet it is a fact of surprising truth that this oddly matched pair came to an abiding understanding that was to shape their future, and their children's.

When Addie Mae sat down on a chair she had dusted and cleaned for years she was a divorced wife of the man sitting across from her. When she rose she was still divorced from him, but she had put forward a proposition which he had accepted—that she should come back and continue as his wife.

Seven years later, when asked why she chose this seemingly inconsistent course, she said, 'For the children's sake.'

For her own sake she had secured a divorce.

For her children's sake she ignored the freedom that divorce bestowed on her.

Such a woman certainly had an unusual domestic outlook. In the light of the outcome perhaps it is not truly surprising that it became deadly.

Addie Mae had escaped from a life that had grown repellent to her. She had secured her freedom from conditions that had amounted to her near-bondage in the mid-twentieth century. Yet the freed Addie Mae was a stranger to herself, one who had the former Addie Mae's responsibilities to her children.

She felt compelled to don her doffed chains. Whatever justification she had contrived to appease her self-anger, she must have felt defeated in her heart. If her marriage had become a mockery from which she had to flee, then how much more of a mockery must her self-induced relationship with a man to whom she was no longer married have seemed to her when in sober earnestness she considered what she had done with her life!

A second rebellion would surely find expression in action more direct and final than the incantations of a mumbling divorce court judge.

So it proved in the event.

Louis matched his wife's willingness to return as his paramour with a fresh desire to please. He moved house. He took his children and their mother to the Belledeau area, which is in Avoyelles Parish, where Cajuns like himself followed the furrows made by a plough, picked cotton in some of the best cotton-growing soil in the world, went fishing in rivers and creeks teeming with fish, or hunting in forests and upland woods where antlered bucks lived in dappled gloom.

Louis still earned his wife's keep by wielding an axe and logging, and by hiring out as a farmhand. They didn't live fancy, but there was enough on the table, and when the days grew chill there was a bright blaze in the hearth.

Again routine settled over the Lemoines. Again Addie Mae found herself enduring the lengthy silences imposed by her husband's affliction. At this stage in her life she could not even be sure whether, as a girl of fifteen, she had married him as much out of pity as to escape her own humdrum life.

Whatever her motives had been, they became confused in perspective. She could not share her husband's introspective spells. They met on no common ground save the demands of everyday living and a forced tenderness bred of sexual sharing and an intimate knowledge of each other's bodies.

Inevitably it was not enough.

Louis's disappearances into the wilderness with his gun became more frequent. Addie Mae found fresh resentment in the fact that the move to Belledeau had done nothing to change fundamentally a life that afforded her no happiness.

She was divorced and yet not divorced. She came to have the belief that no divorce could mean anything to her while Louis lived. Only his death could bring a real divorce for her; while he lived she would never truly be free.

Moreover, she was facing middle age. When she looked in the mirror she saw lines in a face that she had known laugh more easily. In days when that face had no lines. In the spring of 1962 she was thirty-five. She had been married twenty years, been a divorced woman for seven, seen her children grow up, change, become young adults.

She had seen too many changes, and yet not enough change. That was the irony that pervaded her thoughts. In April, 1962, those thoughts took shape, for an idea had grown in her mind and become an obsession.

Addie Mae the Cajun woman, with her inbred fears and dark longings and inverted loyalties, was not mentally geared to combat obsession. She could merely become a victim of her predatory thoughts and submit to their insistent urging towards violence.

When she finally submitted she became calmer.

It was a deadly calm that pervaded the small two-bedroomed home, the rent of which took a fair slice of Louis's weekly wages, in the last days of April and the first week of May. When neighbours asked where Louis was Addie Mae said he had gone off on one of his hunting trips.

But after two weeks' absence his brothers didn't believe it. One of them went to see Sheriff Didier.

It was May 7th.

He told the sheriff: 'Louis always let one of us know when he'd be away for a spell and when he'd be coming back. Now he's been gone two weeks and no word from him. We think something's happened to him.'

Sheriff Didier began making inquiries about the absent man.

A stocky, clean-shaven man with a firm chin and an easy smile, a man who favoured pale soft-brimmed hats and dark suits, the sheriff learned that Louis Paul Lemoine was believed to have left home at seven o'clock in the morning of April 23rd. The hour was not unusual, for the missing man usually left home at that time in his car to drive to Hessmer, where he was employed by a local logging contractor. But it was unusual for Louis to leave without his car, and on April 23rd that was what he had done. He had set off on foot for the Echo-Hessmer highway.

If Louis Paul Lemoine had set out for work that morning it meant he had several miles to walk.

If he hadn't, then why had he not informed one of his brothers of where he was going, since that was a habit of many years, indeed since his boyhood?

The reason for telling one of his brothers was obvious. If the deaf mute had an accident he could not call for help or make himself heard except by firing his gun. After an unusual lapse of time someone would come looking for him.

That had never been necessary, but the boyhood precaution was maintained.

What was peculiar was the fact that Louis would only inform one of his brothers *where* precisely he was heading for when he went hunting. Not his wife or any of his children. Again a custom left over from childhood had become a patterned way of life.

Sheriff Didier went to Hessmer and asked the logging contractor if he knew where Lemoine had gone.

'No,' said the irate employer. 'He knew we were fixed to start a new logging operation that morning. I'll have something to tell Lemoine when he shows. He left me short-handed.'

Which, Sheriff Didier learned, was not in character. Lemoine had not behaved in this way before. Previously when he had gone off for several days' hunting on his own it had been either in a slack season or between logging jobs.

The sheriff called on Addie Mae.

When she appeared at the door of the small house she looked haggard, as though she had slept little during the past nights. She was a small woman, her hair not so fair as it had been when she married Louis, but it was still parted neatly on the right, and her chin-line was still lean, her cheek-bones rather high. She was neat in her person. She wore a broad candy-striped dress with large pale buttons and a black, square-buckled, shiny belt. Over the dress she wore a woollen cardigan. She looked composed but tired. She did not seem surprised at the questions her caller began asking.

Her husband's fishing tacklc was still in the house, but his single-barrel shotgun was missing.

'He was always squandering money on guns and shells,' she said in a tone of tired patience.

'What calibre is the gun that's missing, Mrs. Lemoine?' her caller asked.

He was told a .410 bore. He was also informed that it was her fourteen-year-old son who had told his mother that the gun was missing from its place in the house.

'I don't know anything about guns,' Addie Mae told the sheriff, 'but the boy often goes hunting with his pa.'

'Is the gun's ammunition missing, Mrs. Lemoine?'

She explained that four of the children were still young enough to live at home, so their father did not keep live ammunition around in the house.

'He always keeps the shells for his gun in the locked trunk of the car,' she told the sheriff.

She was asked for the car keys and handed them over. In the locked boot was a full box of .410 shells.

Later that day a conference was held in Marksville, the local parish seat, which was about a dozen miles from Belledeau. The district attorney, J. Roy, pointed out that men had been lost previously in the swamp-lands around Belledeau, but it was reasonable to suppose that someone would have seen Lemoine on his way to the swamp. Folks around Belledeau were all early risers.

The sheriff said he would continue his inquiries. In all some twenty persons were questioned, most of whom gave the same account of the missing man and his moody, anti-social ways, though it was usually agreed he was a good worker. May slipped into June and it was suddenly high summer. On the 4th, Sheriff Didier was sitting in his shirt-sleeves in his Marksville office when he was informed Mrs. Lemoine was outside asking to see him.

'Show her right in,' he said, getting out of his chair.

Addie Mae came in, trim, sad-eyed, and rather frail-looking.

'I've heard from Louis,' she said, producing from her handbag a soiled envelope.

Didier took it, turned it over, and saw that it was addressed to the eldest Lemoine boy and franked with a Baton Rouge post stamp. But to the sheriff's sharp eyes the handwriting looked more like a woman's than a man's.

'Your husband wrote this?' he said casually.

'Oh, no,' she denied quickly. 'This is from the boy's aunt. She lives in the state capital. But read the letter, Sheriff, and you'll know why I brought it.'

The letter, dated May 26th, was a chatty epistle announcing that the aunt looked forward to a proposed visit from her nephew. One passage read:

> 'Your daddy was down here a few days ago, and he said to send you and the other children his love when I wrote. I suppose he'll be returning to you and your mother soon now.'

'You'd better leave this with me, Mrs. Lemoine,' Didier said, holding up the letter.

When Addie Mae had gone he took the letter to the district attorney's office and handed it to Roy.

'What do you think about the handwriting?' he asked.

Neither man was a handwriting expert. But then it did not require a professional calligraphist to appreciate that the hand which had written the envelope had not penned the letter inside it.

'We'll have to get a sample of Addie Mae's writing,' Roy agreed.

'Here it is,' Didier said, putting a fresh piece of paper before the district attorney. It was a briefly worded permission for the sheriff to show the first letter to anyone concerned with his present inquiry. 'I took the precaution to ask her for it,' he explained.

The two sheets of paper were held side by side. The similarities in the handwriting were very readily apparent.

'Begins to look like Louis won't be coming back on his own feet,' the district attorney said harshly.

From notes taken on the previous round of inquiries one item seemed now of special interest. Apparently Addie Mae had gone to a store, the day before Lemoine left home, and asked for some sandwich meat. She had omitted to mention the fact when later interviewed.

'Looks like she purposely didn't refer to that visit,' Roy decided. 'Better check again, Sheriff.'

The storekeeper remembered the visit because he had been interested in the news of Louis Paul Lemoine's disappearance. He told two of the sheriff's men who called on him: 'I remember it for another reason, too. Just as Addie Mae was about to leave she hesitated and turned back. She asked for a couple of shotgun shells. Well, I don't ever recall being asked for just a couple of shells before. Sure, I sell shells from boxes, but just two—well, I asked her if Louis was so good he'd go hunting with only a couple of shells for his gun.'

'What calibre?' asked one of the sheriff's men.

'I remember that also,' the storekeeper nodded. 'She wanted a couple of .410 shells.'

The two sheriff's officers continued on their way from the store to the Lemoine house. It had a plank-floored porch with a couple of steps leading up to it. On the porch was a straight-backed chair and a shiny new washing machine.

Addie Mae was about to start putting the family wash into the machine when the two visitors stepped on to the porch.

'In the warm weather,' she explained with a shy smile, 'I like to work outside.'

The men nodded. One of them took the familiar envelope from his pocket.

'We've brought you back the letter your boy received from his aunt in Baton Rouge,' he said. As the woman reached for the envelope he added, 'Oh, by the way, there is just one thing, Miss Lavespere.' The use of her maiden name was deliberate. 'We'll be contacting the boy's aunt. Thought you ought to know.'

Addie Mae's hand dropped. She had not taken the letter.

She said quietly: 'That won't be necessary. I think you already know what you'll be told. The letter my son received said nothing about Louis being in Baton Rouge. That letter I showed the sheriff was written by me, I wanted you all to think my ex-husband was still alive.'

The last words rang like a knell. But Addie Mae was past caring.

She pointed a finger at the padlocked door of the wash-shed from which she had taken the washing machine.

'You'll find Louis there, beneath the wash-house. I put him in his grave the day after Easter, after I shot him with one of the shells I bought the night before at the general store.'

She suddenly looked like a woman who had been relieved of a great mental burden. When the two sheriff's officers returned to Marksville she accompanied them as their prisoner. In the Marksville jail she was formally charged with murder. She admitted the crime, and told the district attorney that she had shot her divorced husband following one of those curiously held domestic arguments she and the deaf mute had engaged in.

'It was the last straw,' she said in her tired voice.

Sheriff Didier took his men back to Belledeau, where they moved the wash-shed and began digging. Louis Paul Lemoine's body was found about two feet under the ground. The dead man had been neatly wrapped in a sheet and several blankets. His hands were crossed on his chest. There was a hole under the left ear.

The coroner, Dr. Kaufman, had the body transported to a Baptist chapel in the town of Alexandria and arranged for a post mortem to be held. Meanwhile Addie Mae was sitting in her jail cell writing a confession. While a clinical pathologist named Uhrich was deciding that Louis Paul Lemoine had died of a shotgun wound in the side of the head that had resulted in a fractured skull and fatal haemorrhaging, the woman who had contrived her own shotgun divorce was writing:

'Louis (my husband) had argued with me on Easter Eve because I wouldn't go to the dance with him the night before. Late Sunday evening I went to the store and bought some lunch material and also bought two .410 shotgun shells. I had made up my mind to kill Louis, then kill myself.'

After describing a call she made and the trip home she went on:

'After supper I bathed the children. They watched television for a while and went to bed. I then took a bath and sat down in the front room with Louis. At 9 p.m. Louis went to bed, lying on his left side. I don't know if he was asleep or not. The more I looked at him the more I hated him. There was no light on in the room where Louis was. I had tried to go to bed, but Louis wouldn't let me. I was sitting on the sofa in the adjoining room when I decided to get the gun. I went to the cupboard, picked up the .410 bore shotgun. I had gone to the kitchen first to get the shells out of the cabinet. I put one shell in the gun and held the other in my hand. I went to the bedroom where Louis was. I climbed over the foot of my bed so he wouldn't see my shadow on the wall. I don't remember when I cocked the gun. I walked to the bed where Louis was, put the barrel of the gun about six inches from his head, and pulled the trigger. I then put a blanket around the gun, ran out of the house, and stopped by a bush. I intended to shoot myself, but I lost my nerve. I still had the shell that wasn't fired in my hand. I saw a car in a lane close to my house so I ran back to the wash-house, put the gun there, and put the shell in the bottom of a cedar robe. I walked the floor and wringed my hands trying to decide what to do. I finally decided I had to bury Louis or hide his body.'

So far the confession, told in a crisp, clipped style, had brought her to the brink of her greatest ordeal, more poignant than where she turned in the general store and asked for the murder shells, more terribly dramatic even than climbing over a bed to avoid a telltale shadow on a wall and then shattering the bedroom silence with the blast of the shotgun. Her hand was less steady, and her writing progress slower, as she penned:

> 'I went to the bed where Louis was lying. I saw blood on the sheet. So I rolled him up in the sheet and a blanket, and then rolled him off the bed on a quilt and pillow I had put on the floor. I then rolled him up in the quilt and pulled him from the bedroom through the house to the wash-shed. I rolled him to the back of the wash-house and put the washing machine and tubs in front of him so no one could see him. I then closed the wash-house door and made a latch for it so no one could come in. I then put a chair against the door. I went in the kitchen and made some coffee. My son and his friend came in about 5.30, drank some coffee and went to bed. I got them up at about 7.30, when the mother of my son's friend came for him. I sent the other children to school, then went to the wash-shed, took up three boards from the floor, sawed two supports with a buck saw so that I would have room to dig a grave. I then took my shovel and dug a shallow grave, rolled Louis into it and covered him up. I then put the boards back in place. I had removed the washing machine and the rug from the wash-house floor and burned the rug because it had blood on it. I replaced it with one that was on the back porch.'

This human document, with its story of hate and despair and erupting violence, was signed, somewhat curiously, 'Addie Mae Lemoine Lavespere'—witnessing to a cycle of broken hopes: she had been a Lavespere who became a Lemoine who reverted to being a Lavespere.

She was taken to the East Louisiana State Hospital, where the clinical director, Dr. Victor Weiss, arranged for his staff psychiatrists to give her a number of tests that in their opinion would establish her sanity or insanity.

Their findings revealed that the subject of the tests 'understands the usual, natural, and probable consequences of her actions, and has the capacity to understand the charges against her'.

In short, Addie Mae was sane.

That wasn't telling Addie Mae anything she didn't know. The Cajun woman with the dark smouldering eyes and lean chin-line knew very well why she had murdered the man she had divorced and then lived with.

The deaf mute had been her Fate, from the time when, at fifteen, she had learned in some personal way how to communicate not only words but feelings to him. He had offered all she would ever find of romance, and he had presented an open door to another life.

Then the door had slammed shut on her, and she had grown afraid and rebellious and desperate. But divorce had not really re-opened that slammed door. She had gone back, coerced by her mixed feelings for a man who was less than a man and was growing less, as it seemed to her, each year. She saw the children leave home, find the escape that to her had been an illusion. She had tried to seek an emotional outlet in quarrels and harsh wrangling, in denials and bickering. All she had achieved was to discover nothing would save her except death. That discovery also destroyed her.

Her trial opened on October 15th, 1962, a dismal grey Monday, in Marksville. It never really got under way, which produced an anticlimax for the thousand men and women squashed into the limited space of the court-room. The district attorney was known to be ready to demand the death penalty, which would be a challenge to an all-male jury, as is demanded by Louisiana law for all murder trials. But before District Attorney Roy could start presenting his case there was swift consultation at the table of the defence counsel who had been appointed by the court. A fresh plea was entered on the prisoner's behalf.

'Guilty as charged, without capital punishment.'

The court accepted the new plea.

On October 20th Addie Mae Lemoine Lavespere, as she thought of herself, returned to hear the sentence of the court. She was to spend the remainder of her life in the Louisiana State Penitentiary for Women.

For the last time a door had closed on the Cajun woman who had never been sure what to do with freedom except place it in jeopardy.

5 * A Bride for Death

Few women in the history of crime have a record for wanton violence and callous disregard for others to equal that of lovely Grete Beier. She was pale to the point of being ethereal-looking. She was not only a calculating *femme fatale*. She was a calculating murderess.

She was dressed as a bride when she knelt down and placed her head on a block, to await the down-swing of the headsman's sword. It has been said that she never looked lovelier than on that midnight of her execution.

She was twenty-three.

She was the daughter of a burgomaster of a town in Saxony. Born in 1885, she was brought up in cultured surroundings and from her earliest months enjoyed the fruits of civilized living and the benefits of status. She was induced to read those books which were considered at the time to be improving for the minds of maidens. She was set copy-book examples by parents who were fond of her but refused to dote. She was carefully directed into those paths that led to the good life that was the hallmark of Christian gentility. Money, abiding care, cautious love, a happy home life—the benefits deriving from such blessings were hers. For all the difference they made to a child destined to go her own sweet violent way to perdition she might as well have been born in a slum of parents who failed to cherish her as a heaven-sent joy to light their home.

She was a rebel.

She refused to learn by precept. She devoted her life and her energies to indulging her personal desires and fulfilling her wayward longings. The home from which she stepped forth to find a world of her own was a place she derided and mocked with cold contempt.

She had the face and form of a saint. Under the façade lurked a spirit of evil, for the fair Grete was evil. She knew it, she helped to fashion the evil that she exerted and exuded, quite deliberately, so that the very exercise of evil gave her pleasure.

She even found pleasure in murdering her own children, for she had learned the secret of stifling remorse. Not many women share that terrible gift, but Grete Beier had it in abundance. Her criminal tendencies revealed themselves while a schoolgirl. She proved impossible for her governesses to manage. She was sent to a strictly conducted school for young ladies. But Grete Beier had no intention of being a young lady in any restrictive sense.

She managed to escape through the tall gates of the seminary and join a young man whom she had met when with a friend. She was absent for several days while the other girls in the school discussed her escapade in bated whispers. She was found, brought back, and her father summoned.

'You must remove your daughter from this seminary, Herr Beier,' the agitated burgomaster was informed.

It was an ultimatum to the father. To the wayward daughter with the polished blue eyes it seemed that she had learned a secret of high value. One did something and let others worry about the consequences. As the foundation stone for a philosophy based on love of self and self-indulgence it appealed to the immature girl as admirable.

She left the school for young ladies with her resolve hardening.

Herr Beier might have achieved more success in handling his wilful daughter had his wife been more helpful. The truth was that Frau Beier changed in her attitude towards her daughter as the girl grew older. The result was, in the long term, an unhappy one for Grete, for she saw how her acquired charm, allied to her youthful beauty, could sway people towards being sympathetic to her, no matter how outrageous her behaviour.

It was so with Frau Beier.

The mother who had been so careful and correct in the first

formative years of her daughter's life now developed a secret indulgence towards what she considered Grete's whims. Out of hearing of her husband she tried to get down to her daughter's less responsible level of daily comportment and view the world through the eyes of a youth she had lost and never ceased regretting.

The quick-witted girl, able to perceive where advantage to herself lay in this newly developing relationship with her mother, was very ready to use the ill-timed new indulgence for her more secret ends.

She pretended to confide in her mother while using her alleged understanding of girls and their maturing fancies to further her arrangements for secret meetings outside the home and for protracted assignations that were not mentioned to the busy burgomaster. Indeed, there grew up a strange unexpressed conspiracy of silence in Herr Beier's very conservative Saxon home. Mother and daughter were parties to a plot ensuring that he remain in ignorance of his daughter's heel-kicking.

For a while Frau Beier comforted herself with the thought that most indulgent mothers find sooner or later for a mental salve. She was helping Grete to grow up. A girl was not expected to have the high spirits shown by boys. But that did not mean nature never endowed them with any. Far otherwise. She looked back to her lost youth and saw it through a rosy glow of false understanding. When Grete grew older she would not have a heart filled with regrets, and she would have her mother to thank.

It was a beautiful but pathetic illusion. Poor Frau Beier never came to the harsh reality of her daughter's selfish nature. Only one person genuinely mattered in Grete's world—Grete.

Even when she conspired to trap a youth with her beauty and subtle teasing, to make him swear undying affection for her, Grete was calculating. The game of winning soul-sighing lovers was too easy. She used her wiles upon them like a pupil going through exercises. She learned how to inflame the amatory male, how to bring him to the brink of emotional despair and remain too aloof to share in the whirlpool she had set in motion. Like so many sensuous and predatory females before her, she quickly discovered that young men are, by very reason of their lack of years and limited emotional experience, shallow. She refused to see that shallows can become depths. She was a girl growing into a lovely young woman and she was in a hurry to taste life to the full.

She stole money from her father. With the money she bought clothes more suited to an older and more sophisticated woman. Adding to her years by such changes in her appearance as these clothes and fresh hair-dos and some pieces of jewellery afforded, she looked for adventure with older men.

Events conspired to accelerate her maturity.

Frau Beier had become tired of watching her daughter's beauty deepen and listening to her carefully edited versions of meetings with adoring young men, all of whom were chivalrous and courteous and ready to take her home without question when their novelty for her palled.

She felt that in some degree the metamorphosis she was witnessing take place in her daughter could also change her humdrum life. For humdrum it had certainly become after a few months of sharing her daughter's narrated excitements. She looked outside her home for her own beckoning adventure.

Because she was the burgomaster's wife, because she was a woman of settled status in the community, she did not have to look long. At a friend's house she met a suave man of the world, well dressed, with charming manners, and time to dawdle while bestowing soft glances on Frau Beier.

In the middle-aged mother's eyes Herr Merker assumed an aura of pure romance.

What she didn't know, and wasn't likely to be told by the smirking Merker, was that he was very well aware that she had a lovely daughter. So far he had been unable to meet the young woman who was a topic for appreciative discussion among men who considered themselves wise in the ways of women and wantons.

The foolish woman devised a means of inviting Merker to her home without arousing her husband's suspicions.

'I want you to meet Herr Merker,' she told her daughter with a blend of naiveté and cunning that promptly aroused that young female's lively interest.

The outcome was, of course, foreseeable except to the mother, who had put scales over her own eyes. The young woman groping towards sophistication and worldly experience was herself snared by the blandishments of a practised rogue male. It was only a short time after meeting the lady-killer in her mother's company that Grete was meeting him secretly. Too late Frau Beier realized how she had been tricked by her more attractive daughter. When she tried upbraiding the girl she was confronted by a bland stare.

'Why, Mother, what would Father say?'

The question was unanswerable. Anything Herr Beier said would be unwelcome in his unhappy and deluded wife's ears.

'You must give him up, Grete, stop seeing him,' the mother persisted.

'Why?'

'Because he is too old for you, and because I say so.'

Neither reason appealed to Grete Beier as eminently satisfactory. She was sixteen. She continued to meet Merker, and when he took a new apartment she visited him there. Frau Beier feared that the good people of Brand would soon come to learn of the deceit being practised by the burgomaster's daughter, that there would be a scandal, that her daughter's shameless exploitation of her mother's temporary folly would make the Beiers the town laughing-stocks.

It was a prospect too uncomfortable to be endured stoically in secret. Frau Beier required solace of some kind. She sought it from a bottle, which became the first of a long procession of similar bottles.

In fact, she emptied them with alarming ease. She even acquired skill at depleting their contents. By that time she was a committed secret drinker.

Grete quickly took advantage of her mother's hidden vice. She induced her to lie about her daughter's absence from home on certain nights.

'She is staying with one of her friends,' she would tell her husband.

As long as his wife knew of his daughter's comings and goings the burgomaster was satisfied. After all, he wanted to be satisfied, for he understood that Grete was a difficult girl, but then he tried to excuse the little he knew about her on the ground that she was at a difficult age.

The parents of Grete Beier, in their separate ways, were very good at deluding themselves into believing what they wanted to believe and seeing only what they wished their eyes to encounter. Of course, in the case of the mother, she was helped by the bottles of schnapps. But her husband absorbed himself in his municipal affairs with the contained frenzy of a drug addict with a plentiful supply of drugs.

Their child had at least inherited her parents' devotion to whatever she was doing. In place of a challenging occupation or a bottle of strong waters she had Merker, and the lady-killer was completing one side of her education that her parents had no idea had been started.

However, for all his capacity as a lavish lover, Merker had depths unsuspected by his young mistress. He seemed to have a plentiful supply of money without the need for occupying himself with anything so menial or demanding as a job with regular hours. He was a man of leisure who dressed well, and had all the time to devote to his laughing Grete that she could wish. Life was one enthralling round of pleasure.

And pleasure never palled on Grete. She could absorb it like a sponge does water.

The inevitable happened. The day dawned when Grete discovered that she was pregnant. The horrible truth angered her, but she was not dismayed.

Merker appeared to be amused at the news.

'What did you expect, my love?' he said, smiling.

'What shall I do?' she countered.

'Talk to your mother. She can be very useful, my pet.'

Merker was no fool. He had weighed up the negative qualities of his mistress's mother, and understood that in a crisis she could keep her tongue from wagging. Moreover, such silence might even be exploited.

Frau Beier, suddenly sobered by the news brought by her daughter, reacted precisely as Merker had supposed she would.

'You must not have this baby,' she told her daughter, and made her own arrangements for helping to destroy her unborn grandchild.

However, the potions were not effective. Grete was healthy and nature seemed determined to endow her with motherhood despite her efforts to resist fulfilment. The baby was born to a young mother of seventeen who hated it. The child was only hours old when Grete Beier callously smothered it with a pillow. Far from being appalled by what she had done, she gave herself to consideration of the best way to dispose of the small corpse. No reaction set it. No fear clouded her mind to blur the edges of her determination.

Just risen from a bed of confinement, Grete Beier wrapped the body in a shawl, and took it with her when she left the house after dark. When she returned the shawl was neatly folded under her cloak.

She had run the gamut of motherhood and murder, and remained quite unscarred by the significance and meaning of her actions. She was anxious only to return to the course of a life that had been interrupted.

Almost at once Merker, who had helped in keeping her motherhood and her crime a secret shared only by Frau Beier, broke news of financial disaster. His resources were gone. He was well-nigh penniless. He explained that he had been living on the proceeds of several daring forgeries.

'The police were after me, so I came to Brand,' he explained. 'Now it's your turn to provide for us, my love.'

'But I have no money.'

'Your family has,' she was reminded.

'No,' she said. 'I could not ask money of my father.'

'I wasn't thinking of asking.'

'I stole from him once. There would be no second chance.'

Merker shrugged. He did not seem unduly worried.

'If we can't go to your family, then it is up to you,' he said firmly.

'How do you mean?'

Explaining completed yet another phase of Grete Beier's worldly education. She had survived his deception and the discovery that the man of charming ways, the intrepid lover, was a common swindler. She was to survive his willingness to turn pimp.

He took her away from Brand, set her up in a place of her own, and eventually paid the bills incurred with the money she received from a number of wealthy merchants and well-to-do young ne'er-do-wells who visited her and were prepared to be generous in return for the favours she allowed them.

Within a very short while Grete Beier, who had now made a complete break with her family, was established as a successful high-class prostitute. She adapted herself to the demands of such a life with a thoroughgoing determination worthy of a vastly higher calling. She even feigned being in love with a succession of moneyed clients who were kept as a kind of amorous retinue to a lovely young woman who was something of an enigma to the men who made love to her and a very satisfactory source of ready income to the conniving Merker, who had introduced her to the oldest profession.

As an experienced man of the world, as well as the underworld of his day, Merker probably knew that the prostitute's natural demand for some male on whom she could lavish anything she might consider as her own freely bestowed affection would ensure Grete remaining his chattel as long as he used her gently. He took her cash and used her with gentleness, considering it a fair bargain.

But another day of crisis dawned.

Merker, wearing a look of strain, told her that he needed more money or this time he would be unable to keep out of jail. Moreover, he wanted the money in a hurry. Grete had given him all she had, and his pockets were empty.

'You'll have to revise your ideas,' he told her. 'This time there's only your family. Unless you want me in jail, and with me in jail you'd have no protection, my love.'

Grete Beier was not the same young woman of a few months before who had vetoed his suggestion of robbing her father. Her way of life had coarsened her beyond moral redemption. She had lived too long with a smooth-tongued criminal. She had cheated and lied in her efforts to empty men's pockets and to induce them to part with gifts. She could not falter now. Just as she could not endure the thought of not having Merker available. The man had become an integral part of her life in his own poisonous fashion.

She went to Brand and called on her mother, and quickly came to the point. She wanted the key to her father's safe.

'I'll see you get something to keep you well supplied with schnapps,' she promised cynically.

It is possible that Frau Beier tried to argue her daughter away from her resolve. If so, she failed. Certainly she was by this time no equal contestant in a duel of wills. Grete secured the key she wanted, and from her father's safe removed jewellery and a cheque-book. Within hours of the robbery, Merker, the skilled forger who had been supplied with a copy of Herr Beier's signature, had withdrawn every pfennig from the burgomaster's bank account.

Anxious that the theft should not be traced to herself, and probably equally anxious that her mother should not be questioned too strenuously, the thief set about turning suspicion towards an innocent person.

She had a duplicate key of her father's safe cut, and went visiting a friend of the Beier family with her mother. When the friend was absent from the room Grete concealed the duplicate key behind a drawer in a side table.

It was days later that the burgomaster went to his safe and discovered his loss. Frau Beier, who had been coached by her determined daughter, flutteringly admitted having seen her friend examining the safe when she was last in the house. The burgomaster went to the police who called on the woman now suspected of being concerned in the robbery. She protested her innocence most strenuously, but when the searching police found the hidden key her protests were of small avail. She was arrested.

However, she was cleared of the charge in unexpected fashion. The maid she employed was more nosy than her mistress realized. While Frau Beier and her daughter had been alone in the room where the key was found the servant had peered at them through a keyhole. She had seen Grete Beier opening the drawer of the side table. She had thought little of it until her mistress was placed under arrest and she heard why.

Justice now took its stern course. The innocent woman was freed and Grete Beier was arrested, charged with having stolen the jewellery and cheque-book from her father. The scandal in the provincial German town, with its narrow-minded outlook and readiness to condemn those so-called betters who had been found erring, resulted in the complete collapse of the outraged burgomaster. He didn't recover for a very long while.

Meanwhile Grete reposed in jail, awaiting her trial. But she could not be said to languish. She wrote a note to Merker—who had remained concealed in the wings, as it were, while the recent Beier family drama unfolded—in which she instructed him to go to the home of the nosy maid, chloroform her, then strangle her to prevent her appearing as a witness at the forthcoming trial. The letter with this planned murder outlined was hidden in the hem of a blouse. The blouse was included with some clothes she had packed to be sent to her mother to have washed. However, a wardress diligently examined the dirty clothes, and felt the stiffened section of hem. The note was removed, and Grete was charged with the additional crime of incitement to murder.

The story was released, Merker hurriedly removed himself, and Grete was isolated. In court she appeared, it is said, demure and even sad. But she was an actress able to play most roles convenient to her, and she was a woman in a world where the males were in charge of the law. Perhaps it was the demure and sad look that kept her sentence down to five years. If so, then the lesson learned in court explains why she became a model prisoner. The officials reported that she was a completely changed person. The nuns who visited her confirmed the change and expressed the opinion that she was quite reformed. The authorities decided to set the seal of their approval on the good work done by prison discipline by releasing their reformed felon.

She went to the Beiers' new home in Chemnitz, for her father, after recovering his health, had resigned as burgomaster of Brand. But the novelty of being the daughter of a respected family once more quickly wore threadbare. Grete had learned too much from Merker, come to know ways of living that appealed more strongly to her nature, and it was not long before she was looking for male companionship.

She met a young engineer named Pressler who spoke to her of his ambitions. Pressler was utterly captivated by the lovely young woman. He wanted to marry her, and marriage was what Herr Beier wanted most ardently for his daughter. He had the naive belief of some fathers who lack understanding that the matrimonial state would complete what he looked upon as her cure. Grete was no invalid suffering from a malady. She was a criminal living through an interlude between crimes. That interlude ended when Merker reappeared. He had heard of her release from jail, and had traced her to Chemnitz, and he remained under cover until he knew what was happening. He chose to show himself to Grete a short while before her intended marriage to the engineer.

It was as though the pair had not been parted. The evil they shared proved to be a bond stronger than forged steel. She obtained samples of an aged uncle's signature, and Merker forged a will in which the ailing relative's total possessions were left to his beloved niece. But the old man obstinately clung to life, and Merker refused to consider murder because of Grete's past record.

Grete decided Pressler must provide the cash required, and that he would have to die. She copied the love letters she had received from him and destroyed the originals. By this time she was confident she could imitate his handwriting sufficiently well to deceive a casual reader. Excited because she had not asked Merker to help her, she went ahead with her scheme.

On the day of the Freiburg Fair she told some friends, 'I will have to go back to Chemnitz early because my uncle is coming from Paris and my father wants me to prepare the dinner.'

It was a lie. She had no uncle in Paris. In Chemnitz she met Pressler, and went with him to his apartment. She allowed him the intimacies of a fiancé without informing him that she had a pistol and a phial of potassium cyanide in her pocket.

She was more or less truthful when she told him: 'I've brought you a present from the fair. Close your eyes.'

Playfully she tied a cloth around his head.

'Say something, darling,' she said.

Pressler opened his mouth to speak, but before he could utter the first word she had thrust the barrel of the small pistol into his mouth and pulled the trigger. The murdered man fell forward. With no sense of shock his murderess set about the next phase of her plot. On the table near the body she placed a forged will and a suicide note. The will left everything Pressler possessed to the woman he had expected to marry. In a bureau with his other papers she planted for eventual discovery a letter in a different hand purporting to be from an Italian woman who addressed him as her husband. The writer claimed that she had married him in order to avenge her sister, who had been seduced and abandoned by Pressler, by leaving him and then waiting until she could harm him. His engagement to Grete Beier now gave her the awaited opportunity. She offered him two alternatives: a charge of bigamy if he married the German woman or suicide. The choice was his.

Grete Beier had a varied and fanciful imagination, and had not been afraid to call upon it.

She returned by train to Freiburg, rejoined her friends, then sent her mother a wire saying she would not be home until the next day. That night she spent with Merker, to whom she said nothing of the murder or the plot she had worked out.

When Pressler's body was found the authorities did not suspect foul play. Grete, in black and with the sad look back on her lovely face and composed features, received a sum amounting to several hundred pounds, the estate of her fiancé.

The way was cleared for a more prolonged return to Merker's desired company. Most of Pressler's money disappeared in the lady-killer's deep pocket. Merker laughed at the cleverness displayed by his pet.

'You must renew your attentions to your dear uncle who lingers on so obstinately,' he smiled.

Nothing loath, the niece returned to paying visits to the aged relative. It is possible that only one thing prevented his unnaturally early demise. That was the finding by a brother of the dead Pressler of certain discrepancies in his will. It seemed to him a man could not be mistaken in salient facts about his own family. He had inquiries made. The inquiries produced genuine signatures and handwriting specimens, but when Grete Beier was questioned she in turn produced the copied love letters. However, a handwriting expert pointed to basic differences, which, however, were not shown in the letter from the alleged Italian wife.

Again Grete was arrested, this time charged with murder.

Her father suffered another complete collapse. He did not recover. About the time of his funeral, which Grete could not attend, Merker bowed out for the second time. For Grete history was repeating itself. She herself provided one notable change from precedent. She confessed to murdering Pressler. She also told the crowded court, when she appeared on trial, of her life with Merker, to whom, she claimed, she had borne three children.

'I killed them all as soon as they were born,' she told the shocked court in a cold voice empty of any emotion. 'We didn't want children. We wanted to enjoy ourselves.' She told how she had poisoned Pressler's coffee before shooting him. Her utter callousness, and her complete objectivity in relating how she had brought about Pressler's death, hardened the eyes of all who stared at her across the court-room. At one point she was brusque almost to the point of flippancy.

'I took a napkin,' she said, 'and tied it round his head. Why, I don't know, for his eyes were shut. I placed the pistol in his mouth when it opened and pressed the trigger.'

The president of the court asked her with quiet sternness if she felt any horror or remorse for her terrible deed. Her short reply was, 'At the funeral I felt sorry.' It did not even sound true.

She was found guilty and the court sentenced her to death, which at that time, in 1908, meant beheading by a headsman who had been born in Saxony. The executioner, by Saxon custom and ritual, would wear a frock-coat and a white tie. He would wield a two-handed sword, and the law permitted him only one blow at the doomed neck, and that had to fall between dusk and dawn.

A Dresden butcher named Max Ulmfeld was the Saxon State executioner at the time, only six years before Wilhelm the Second sent his Uhlans across the frontier with Belgium and his Chancellor tore up a certain scrap of paper.

Herr Ulmfeld appeared at the door of Grete Beier's cell shortly before midnight and woke her from sleep. She looked at his dark cutaway coat and fresh white tie and knew his purpose even though he was a stranger. She had been told it was customary not to inform a condemned prisoner of the actual date of execution. She was quite composed as, dressed in a gown of bridal white, she walked with her executioner from her cell into the prison courtyard, where a small altar had been draped in black. On the altar was a simple white crucifix. Beyond the altar was a dark desk at which was seated the trial judge and the public prosecutor.

Both judgment and sentence were read to the pale-faced but upright prisoner, and the judge announced that no pardon had been granted. The priest came forward.

'Do you repent, my daughter?' he asked quietly.

There was a most dramatic pause, broken when Grete Beier sank her proud head and whispered, 'Yes.'

She was led to the death block and knelt on the cushion in front of it. Her slender arms were secured with straps to the sides of the wide block. Her eyes stared into the shiny pail that would catch her head. She had not glanced at the dark wooden coffin waiting to receive her butchered remains.

On the stroke of midnight Max Ulmfeld lifted his sword. When its freshly honed edge bit into the tough death block the law had been observed. One stroke only, and the shiny pail was no longer empty.

Also, it was no longer shiny.

6 * Stronger than Love

The course of Mary Blandy's true love for a polished rogue did not only run unsmoothly, it turned into a veritable whirlpool that destroyed her. Yet this young woman who had little hope of being remembered by future generations after she had lived out her normal span of life, not only died on the gallows as the murderess of her father, whom she had professed to love, but she had the distinction—howbeit an unenviable one—of being the first woman to be convicted of murder on evidence provided by a contemporary expert on the nature and properties of a virulent poison.

She was the child of Francis Blandy, a prosperous solicitor who was the town clerk of Henley-on-Thames. The Blandys lived in a large house in London Road, and enjoyed the respect and often the envy of their neighbours. Francis Blandy was liked as a man and his wife was a gracious hostess. Life was lived to a quiet rhythm and a gracious pattern in the first half of the eighteenth century, and the Blandys were typical middle-class people of their time. They looked up to the landed gentry, and in their turn were looked up to by those they considered their social inferiors. The country had withstood the drenching military cloudburst that was Charles Edward Stuart's invasion and foray in 1745 and the American Revolutionary War was a quarter of a century away over the horizon of the future. With seamen and empire builders of the calibre of Captain James Cook about to make the world a smaller place, Britain was preparing to enter the industrial age that was to make her truly great for a century and a half.

For a family of the standing and social status of the Blandys the future seemed highly promising. Indeed, they had only one domestic problem.

They had to find a suitable husband for their daughter Mary. Which should have been no problem at all. For Mary Blandy was a pretty woman with dark eyes and luxuriant brown hair. She had charm and she was cultured. True, she was no fashionable beauty of the London salons, but she was quick-witted, and although she was no blue stocking she had something of far greater appeal to a prospective husband than a brilliant turn of conversation. She had a fortune of some ten thousand pounds in her own right.

Moreover, she could be expected, with every confidence, to inherit in due course the comfortable estate of her father, a man whose knowledge of the law had done little to impede his acquiring a fortune that had brought not only material wealth but social prestige.

In short Mary Blandy was a young lady of the kind that, some years later, Richard Brinsley Sheridan might be looking for to provide a prototype for one of the heroines in his social comedies. Unfortunately for Mary Blandy her choice between the rivals for her affection, father and lover, was the wrong one.

Mainly because she was very much the victim of her own unleashed passion.

It is hard to believe that she had few suitors. With her looks, her family background, her own financial substance, there must have been many sons of Oxfordshire squires ready to ride over to Henley and pay their respects to the brown-haired heiress.

Why she did not marry early was most likely due to parental ambition. The town clerk of Henley might have believed his daughter, with some patience, could achieve a title in the matrimonial stakes. Indeed his daughter marrying a title in the mid-eighteenth century was no far-fetched fatherly dream, and after the upheavals of the past century there were quite a few titles to be exchanged, in the matrimonial sense, for a reasonable supply of cash. Social values were changing with the value of land, and there was no impost on a father's dream.

However that may be, Mary Blandy, born in 1720, did not marry young. But she did look towards a title.

The man she looked at was Captain the Honourable William Henry Cranstoun, fifth son of Lord Cranstoun, a Scottish peer, and nephew of Lord Mark Kerr, who had bought a lavish house near Henley with the equally lavish name of The Paradise. Reports on Captain Cranstoun's physical attractiveness vary with startling discrepancies. It has been claimed that he was young and handsome. It has also been claimed that he was pock-marked and had a noticeable squint, and if indeed he was twenty years older than Mary Blandy then he certainly was not young, but dangerously close to middle age, not always the most attractive years for an eighteenth-century male who believed in good living.

However, handsome or not, young or otherwise, Cranstoun had the military man's swagger, and that was quite something in the Oxfordshire lanes and Thames-side villages. Mary Blandy first met him when she attended a gathering presided over by Lord Mark. At the time she was twenty-six.

Cranstoun was a professional gallant and his airs suggested London and sophistication. The woman approaching thirty, and looking for a man to whom she could give her fortune and devote herself, was enchanted. The word is really fitting. For there can be little doubt that in the months ahead Mary Blandy behaved like a woman on whom a spell has been cast.

She accepted invitations from Cranstoun, she wrote him letters and received endearing missives from him. These days began a roseate period of her life, and when Cranstoun tenderly asked her to become his wife it seemed that the virtue of patience had indeed reaped its just reward.

Apparently there was the tiniest of clouds in the rosy firmament.

With commendable and touching honesty the gallant captain informed his wife-to-be that there was a designing female in London who was posing as his wife and who had deceived not only his friends but some very useful tradesmen. He was making arrangements to see that her imposture was exposed, and was further taking advice to have his position regularized by the courts.

To the daughter of a solicitor it sounded familiar, and perhaps it was this terminology of courts and men of law on Cranstoun's tongue that beguiled her into believing what she had heard was no more than an irregularity that a short delay in achieving ultimate happiness could put right.

She readily agreed that they should say nothing about their affections and intentions of marrying until the outcome of the court action in London.

However, she had been told an edited version of the truth. Lord Mark Kerr, perhaps aware of his obligations as a good neighbour, or believing that The Paradise would not be lost to him if he indulged in a little social fresh air, wrote a confidential letter to Francis Blandy.

It was a most cautiously worded epistle, for Lord Mark was dealing with a lawyer, but it was truthful, a fact that merited much. He wrote that he felt Mr. Blandy should know that his nephew, Captain Cranstoun, was already a man with a wife. She lived in Scotland, with his child.

Francis Blandy was not tardy in securing confirmation. He felt a surging indignation at what he considered the captain's duplicity. The facts, as he had them enlarged for him, related a story two years old. It appeared that Miss Anne Murray, the daughter of a Jacobite family who were staunch Catholics, had caught the roving eye of William Cranstoun. She had also listened to his protestations of undying love. Possibly it was an affair of passion, for the young Scotswoman was very much the social inferior of the man who claimed he wanted to marry her.

Like Mary Blandy, Anne Murray admitted she could find no personal obstacle to marriage with the son of a baron. Acting for once both impulsively and incautiously, William Cranstoun wedded the Scotswoman and lived with her as his wife.

Which was not very long in view of those firm protestations of undying love. In fact, the change in the husband came about when he had a sharp letter from his father, announcing that not only did he disapprove of such a stupid *mésalliance* but his daughter-in-law was neither welcome in his home nor would he acknowledge her in public.

Parental disapproval could only be felt more keenly in one other way. William Cranstoun certainly felt it. His allowance was stopped until he came to his senses, as it was put to him. So at a time in his life when he required money more urgently than ever before he found himself with less.

His undying love became amazingly mortal.

He left the woman about to bear his bairn and journeyed to face his father's ire and sound out the prospects for a renewal of his allowance. It was no case of distance lending enchantment to the view, for upon arriving back among his London friends the married son of Baron Cranstoun decided to explain that there had been a misunderstanding. He had promised to marry Miss Anne Murray, but had not actually done so.

His friends purported to believe the lie. Behind his back they sniggered. His family felt ashamed of the poltroon they had to own was one of them. Shame stirred Lord Mark to write his letter to Francis Blandy.

At the time it arrived at the house in London Road, Henley, Mrs. Cranstoun, in Scotland, was petitioning the Scottish Commissionary Court to have her marriage to Cranstoun declared valid and her child his.

A good many people's principles, it seemed, were undergoing rough treatment.

Anyway, that was what Francis Blandy had to impart to his daughter, a young woman in no mood to receive the information with equanimity. She would not agree to recognize that she had been told a bald inversion of the truth. Any hope Francis Blandy had of persuading her to accept the facts was killed when Cranstoun attempted to save face by calling at the Blandy home. Common courtesy and neighbourliness demanded that he was not kept waiting too long. He was received in a frozen atmosphere, to which he seemed impervious. He had called, he explained, to correct a false impression that had achieved currency much to his chagrin and annoyance. Word had gone round that he was married to a certain Anne Murray. This he stoutly and insistently denied upon his honour as an officer and a gentleman.

At this point in his declamation he looked to the ladies. Both Mary and her mother dimpled at him. He knew his story had gone over there. He looked to the father. Francis Blandy remained stone-faced.

The visitor went on to explain that there had been a certain entanglement, as he described it, with Miss Murray. He regretted it because he now knew that his later emotions were more abiding.

Francis Blandy lost his patience in a hurry. He was quite able, he believed, to perceive a rogue when one stood in front of him and he had the evidence in his own hands to support the charge of roguery. He adopted his official town clerk's manner and told Captain the Honourable William Henry Cranstoun to leave his house and to stop paying court to his daughter.

Captain Cranstoun the military gentleman began an orderly retreat. He smiled on the ladies, bowed, took note of the tears in Mary's eyes, and went out through the front door. As soon as he had gone Francis Blandy found he had mutiny on his hands. It was as though, without a word spoken, his womenfolk were united to attack him and attempt to reverse a decision he had told himself was unalterable.

However, the man of law was practised in the art of effective compromise. He tried a subterfuge because he genuinely believed events would support his belief that Cranstoun was a rogue and a liar.

He told Mary and her mother that he was a reasonable man, which they had given every evidence of doubting, and that if the appeal in Scotland by Anne Murray, who was calling herself Mrs. Cranstoun, to have her marriage ratified was lost, then he would no longer withhold his consent to Cranstoun's paying suit to his daughter.

Mother and daughter looked at each other. The forces arrayed against him could be turned and put to flight, Francis Blandy saw. He seized the moment to add his trenchant stipulation. But if, on the other hand, the Scottish court upheld the appeal, then Cranstoun was in truth a married man according to the law. Until that was known his daughter must not see Cranstoun or communicate with him.

Sobbingly Mary Blandy professed to agree to her father's ultimatum. Her mother led her away. Both women were dabbing their eyes. The Blandy household was not used to such emotional upheavals.

However, Mary was content neither to abide by the terms laid down by her father nor to remain with Cranstoun lost to her. She took the first opportunity she could of writing to him. By return came a letter making a secret assignation. The moment she saw Cranstoun she threw herself into his arms.

Captain the Honourable William Henry Cranstoun smiled down

on her upturned face. He felt he could afford to. He was as good as holding ten thousand pounds in his arms. It was the kind of feeling that allows a tense man to relax, and Cranstoun had been tense for far too long, he considered.

The secret courtship was given a fresh lease of life.

However, as though to help the pair who considered themselves ill-starved lovers, Mary's mother in 1749 suddenly became very ill. When she was on what in truth proved to be her deathbed she told her mournful husband that she could not depart this life happy without setting eyes again on 'my beloved son-in-law', as she referred to Cranstoun.

This was the one stroke dealt by an unsmiling Fate that could bring Francis Blandy to change his resolve. He swallowed his pride and sent an invitation to Cranstoun to stay in the Blandy home for a while. It would pleasure his wife, he was careful to explain.

Cranstoun made a triumphal return and remained throughout several months playing his sorrowing role at the bedside of the dying woman. Mrs. Blandy's last whispered words were to her husband as she grasped his hand in a weak grip.

'Mary has set her heart on Cranstoun. When I am gone let no one set you against the match, Francis.'

The lawyer's face was twisted with emotion. His wife was leaving him for eternity and they both knew it. However, he would not temporize.

'They must wait until the unhappy affair in Scotland is settled.'

It was the man of law speaking. But it was the heart-broken husband who watched his wife take her last breath.

Not long after Mrs. Blandy had been laid to rest in the neighbouring churchyard Francis Blandy received a letter that had been delayed in transit from Scotland. With the letter, written by Mrs. Cranstoun, was a copy of the court's decree declaring her marriage to William Cranstoun legal and binding.

Francis Blandy felt the letter had come too late to save him the nagging remorse at having acted, as he now saw it, perversely towards his dying wife. But there was one person about whom he felt no iota of remorse or any other genuine emotion other than contempt.

He told his daughter that what she considered her engagement to Cranstoun must now be considered irrevocably broken.

'I forbid you to see that man again. He is a scoundrel,' he declared.

Unfortunately Francis Blandy did not treat his daughter of mature age like an adult. He still looked upon her as the child who had been accustomed to accepting her father's decisions as utterly final and had never questioned their wisdom.

Another secret missive was taken to Cranstoun. More clandestine meetings were arranged. The eighteenth century was not so far removed in superstition from the alchemists of the Middle Ages for simple folk not to believe in the efficacy of love potions, in signs and omens, and the potency of stellar influences on human destiny.

When Cranstoun confided that he felt he should procure a powder which might have the power, if administered to Mary's father, of turning his enmity into friendship or even love, she seized upon the suggestion as almost heaven-sent.

Cranstoun needed no more encouragement.

However, Mary Blandy was no simple country lass. She was educated, well read, and she was a grown woman capable of passion. There can be no doubt that she felt extremely hostile towards her father for his continued thwarting of her wishes. She wanted to marry Cranstoun, and in due time it was conceivable she might even become the Baroness Cranstoun, and she did not want to hear about another woman in Scotland who was merely a designing harridan. Nor did she want to hear about the bailiffs who were dunning Cranstoun. Whether the powders were to induce Francis Blandy to change his heart and mind towards Cranstoun did not matter. There had to be some change. It was change that was essential. Without change she could not marry Cranstoun and satisfy her heart's longing.

Mary Blandy, by being continuously frustrated, had grown wilful, and in her wilfulness she became determined.

To demonstrate her determination to effect the necessary change she desired she accepted the powders Cranstoun gave her and fed them to her father surreptitiously in his morning gruel and other dishes, and in his tea.

Francis Blandy took to his bed, suffering acute pains in his intestines. His teeth became loose and he was able to eat only soft food and slops. Life, what was left to him, became a misery to the poor man.

Mary went about the house of which she had been mistress since her mother's death with a cheerful face and pert ways, her step almost blithe. She gave no sign that she expected the potions to change her father's attitude towards the man for whose love she was dipping her hands in murder, as well she knew.

She did not keep up the farce with Cranstoun not around to smile approval at her performance. She kept close watch on her bedridden father, visited him frequently, and attended to preparing his food herself.

On one occasion, which was well remembered later, she confided in one of the servants, 'I'm afraid poor dear Papa will not live much longer.'

A curious comment when one realizes it was not evoked by any questions about the possible outcome of the mysterious illness. But not so curious when one knows that on one occasion when a servant took a sip of a beverage Mary had brewed for her father the girl became very sick. It was this servant, a shrewd girl named Susan, who later took the opportunity of examining a pan in which Mary had warmed some gruel she had taken to her father. Like a white, rather gritty scum, there were dried streaks on the pan's surface. The servant rubbed some off into a powder and kept them.

Apparently Mary could go on deceiving her father, perhaps even herself, but some of the staff of the Blandy household were becoming more than merely suspicious of the daughter's acts and intentions.

Cranstoun came calling and stayed. He and Mary both announced that they had heard rather sepulchral music in the middle of the night. To the local villagers this was a sign that death was about to visit the house. Cranstoun did better. He told some friends in the Henley area that he had seen Francis Blandy's double 'in his white stockings, with his coat on and a cap on his head'. Another sign that Francis Blandy was on the point of departure for a possibly better world.

With the plot thickening as much as the gruels Mary was daily feeding her father, Cranstoun decided to provide himself with a little insurance. The safest seemed to be distance. He went to Scotland.

Some while after kissing him a fond farewell Mary received from him a small parcel containing a number of Scottish pebble ornaments, fashionable gewgaws of the period, together with a white powder for cleaning them. The love-potion pretence was over.

So was any chance of Mary Blandy ever pretending she did not know what she was doing. Instead of using the powder for cleaning the trashy bric-à-brac, she put some in her father's tea. However, she was no Borgia in her poisoning skills. She overdid the dosing, and made the tea so filthy-tasting her father spat it out and refused to drink any more.

She returned to the gruel routine. First she warned the servants against sampling any. She had been annoyed by the girl who had previously been made ill by her curiosity for sampling a sick man's food.

'If you eat any,' said the mistress in a voice of storm, meant to quell any sly resolve to disobey, 'it will do for you.'

Surely a most incautious remark until one reflects that Mary Blandy lived in a household where her word was virtually the law of a feudal overlord. With her father confined to his sick-bed she was the whole Blandy family and she spoke with its unquestioned domestic authority.

It was after spooning some of this fresh gruel into her father's mouth that Mary sat by and watched her father's agonizing collapse. She sent one of the servants to summon a doctor from Reading, who could do little. When he had gone Mary walked into the kitchen and said to the cook, 'If anything should happen, Betty, will you come with me to Scotland?'

The cook stood blinking at her open-mouthed. Clucking her tongue impatiently, the mistress withdrew. The cook, who knew of the white pan scum that had been saved, told the servant who had collected it to show it to the doctor when next he came. The morrow's breakfast gruel for the sick man was prepared by Mary as previously, but this time one of the servants managed to collect a sample. It was given to the doctor, with the white pan scum.

Before the doctor could come to any decision about the samples he had been given there arrived another letter from Cranstoun, exhorting Mary to increase the powder doses, for it must have become apparent to him that the poisoned powders were weak in potency and inefficient. She did so, and her father suffered a terrible vomiting paroxysm. When he subsided he gasped in a drained voice, 'Mary, I was nearly poisoned twenty years ago, and now I am verily poisoned after all.'

The guilty daughter became so scared that her father had divined her guilt that she ran to her room, collected Cranstoun's letters, and threw them, with a small packet, into the fire. Not every particle of the letters was destroyed by the flames. A servant raking over the ashes found one charred fragment containing the words 'Powder to clean the pebbles', written in what was later proved to be Cranstoun's handwriting.

Later that same day Mary wrote a fresh letter to Cranstoun. It began:

> 'My dear Billy,
>
> My father is so bad that, if you don't hear from me soon, don't be frightened. I am better myself. Lest any accident should happen to your letters, take care what you write.'

Hardly the terms one would expect an innocent girl to write. But then guilt was by this time sitting uneasily on her shoulders. She was too flustered to think clearly or discerningly. Not only had she spoken incautiously to several of the servants, but she gave this latest letter addressed to Cranstoun to a chance visitor to post for her. The visitor had been made suspicious by the atmosphere of presumed death pervading the Blandy home. He took a copy of the letter, which he brought to the sick man.

'You must read this, my friend,' he said urgently.

Actually Francis Blandy had been previously warned by one of the servants that it was believed his daughter was poisoning him, but had pretended not to take the warning seriously.

Now he looked at the friend who had brought the copy of Mary's letter and said in his failing voice: 'Poor lovesick little girl. What will a woman not do for the man she loves.'

Therein lies much of the basic tragedy. Even when dying, faced by the harsh truth that he was slowly being murdered,

Francis Blandy still thought of his daughter who was now over thirty as a little girl.

Then was enacted a scene which few theatre audiences would be willing to concede had any element of reality. Yet it was starkest tragedy.

The dying father had a servant summon his daughter. She came into his room rather tremulously, as though aware of what he was about to accuse her of doing. But his manner was so gentle with her, so full of compassion for her criminal folly, that she swiftly saw him as the father she had run to with her troubles when a child. Cranstoun's enchantment was suddenly lifted from her by the sheer pathos of her dying father's kindness.

She fell to her knees at his bedside, crying copiously, and a choked confession spilled from her lips.

'It was he alone who conceived it!' she cried. 'I was his helpless tool, unable to resist him.'

She rose and flung her arms around her father's neck.

'Forgive me,' she begged. 'Tell me that you do forgive me—that you do not curse me.'

The dying man stroked the lush brown hair of his murderess and beloved child.

'I, curse you?' he said in a husky whisper. 'No, I bless you, my child, and hope God will bless you too and amend your life.'

Summoning almost the last of his strength, the dying man of law warned his daughter against further folly. He cautioned her to say or do nothing which could incriminate her.

Then, as though he had performed a final duty for which he had saved his last remaining breath and failing will, Francis Blandy sank back on his pillow and died. A scene that possibly has no parallel in recorded crime annals was over. It was Wednesday, August 14th, 1751.

There remained the final ordeal of the murderess who had received the murdered father's blessing.

On the evidence provided by the doctor a warrant was sworn out and served. She was charged with her father's murder and taken to Oxford in a carriage to await the next Assizes. At the inquest it was established that Francis Blandy had died of arsenical poisoning. The samples given the doctor had contained arsenic and arsenic had been found in the dead lawyer's stomach at a post mortem.

Mary Blandy's trial for murdering her father by administering arsenic to him was held in the Divinity School at Oxford. It opened on a bright day when the countryside over which some of the sharpest skirmishing in the Civil War of a hundred years before had been made was glowing with colour through the soft river mists.

The court was crowded, and the sentiment of those who listened eagerly to the evidence was sharply divided. There were those who believed Mary Blandy to be a sweet, dutiful daughter incapable of the harsh treatment of her father of which she was accused. Others found themselves persuaded by the obvious malice of the two servants, including the girl Susan, who had behaved more like a Bow Street Runner than a country wench paid to clean and scrub. Witnesses came forward to testify warmly to the affection Mary had always shown her father. The defence was direct and sound within its limitations. It maintained that the well-educated daughter of a successful country solicitor believed in love potions, and, moreover, gave the white powders to her father in the firm conviction that she was giving him an old Scots herbal mixture known to warm chill affection.

But it was of small use. The jury was absent five minutes before they returned their verdict of guilty. The prisoner heard herself sentenced to die by hanging.

The one witness who could have helped Mary Blandy had taken the precaution of sailing to the Continent. The not so honourable William Henry Cranstoun, the deserted Mary Blandy's 'Dear Billy', was anxious to save his cravated neck. The neck he had fondled with soft touch could, quite literally, go hang—as indeed it did. But then Cranstoun was adept at placing his inamorati in painful quandaries. It is of passing interest that he died in poverty.

Of more interest perhaps is the irony inherent in the eventual disclosure that Mary Blandy was no heiress possessing ten thousand pounds in her own right. That had been a pleasant fiction of a father over-anxious that his daughter should marry well. Francis Blandy's own estate at the time of his death was not valued at half that sum.

She spent the time before her execution writing to her

friends, many of whom replied to her in warm letters of affection. On the morning she faced the hangman she rose early and dressed in a close-fitting frock of black silk. When the time arrived for her to approach the gallows her step was firm. Her arms were secured with ribbons of Padua silk. It was April 6th, 1752, and there was the fresh scent of spring in the air. The young woman from a country home took her last look at a tree on Castle Green, for her gallows was an improvised affair of a stout pole with ends supported by two apple-trees.

Perhaps those trees, with their soft flush of spring colour, brought peace at last to the tortured mind of the young woman whose love had proved a deadly thing that brought her no true rapture but filled her heart with regrets and bitter remorse.

7 * Invitation to an Ogress

Two years after Grete Beier donned her white bridal array to meet the Saxon butcher-headsman a Paris crowd collected outside the building of the Seine Assize Court, where another multiple murderess had been found guilty, and chanted over and over, 'Death to the ogress.'

If Jeanne Weber, somewhere in the interior of the dour pile of architecture, could have heard them it would have sounded like history repeating itself. For she had heard a mob chant those same words, so that the present was a kind of echo of the past.

But an echo that was to be abruptly broken.

The outcome of her previous trial had been a change of heart on the part of the bloodthirsty mob and an acquittal. Now a die had been cast. There could be no acquittal, as the mob would not undergo another change of heart.

Jeanne Weber was where her blood lust would have to devour itself until her fingers reached for her own throat.

She was a Breton, born of poor parents in the Côtes du Nord. Her father sailed with his fellow-fishermen and returned to live the simple life of a man of those northern coasts. He and his wife had eight children, and there were times when the bread and wine on the family table were not plentiful. There were too many mouths to feed.

Jeanne's one was. The girl grew up to know what it meant to crawl into her bed with a not satisfied stomach, and to awake hungry. She wore drab clothes of dark hues and coarse textures, and her education was primary in the extreme. She was strong physically, but time was to prove that her strength did not extend to her mind.

She seemed a simple girl, willing enough to undertake her share of the tasks childhood imposed on her brothers and sisters, but if she grew up a trifle sly it was excused as shyness. Jeanne was often morose as a child. She seemed to spend hours content with the fancies and fantasies of her own thoughts. Perhaps she was merely subdued by them. Still possibly she could not reach understanding of them or of a strange compulsive longing that must have stirred her by the time she was fourteen and was sent to work as a maid in the house of a local family of good standing.

She lived in, and the break with her former home life was as final as the snapping of a piece of wood. She did not return to the family roof even on a visit. She felt no longing to see her parents. It was almost as though she were afraid of the childhood past from which she had escaped.

When she left the post first found for her she took another, rather similar. But she had no wish to settle down and translate herself into a family retainer. There were other jobs, more new faces that told her she was employed, and with each change it was as though she crept a few kilometres closer to Paris.

By the time she reached the city she was old enough to be thinking of a husband.

It was not long before she found one.

His name was Marcel Weber, and he lived in a run-down working-class district of slum tenements known as the Goutte d'Or, where the only gold that glittered was in the mouths of the women who signed on with the brothel-keepers. Marcel was one of four brothers who worked in the same area, three of whom married girls of the district and bred children who ran about the streets of the Goutte d'Or. Marcel and Jeanne Weber had three children, none of them robust, and only little Marcel survived the rigours of slum childhood.

Marcel, the father, was a steady man who did not get drunk and exercise his frustration with life by beating his Breton wife. He worked as a timekeeper for a transport company, and it was said the firm's clocks could be adjusted to his comings and goings.

Jeanne had grown fond of the grape's fermented juice following the death of two of her children. Her in-laws shook their heads at this sign of what they considered moral weakness, but they felt they had to be indulgent towards the grieving mother. Besides, Jeanne was from Brittany, and they felt superior to the country girl from the provinces.

A typical winter of fogs and sleet and dark afternoons dragged the New Year 1905 into March, a month when blustery winds could remind the wife from Brittany of the keen breezes of the Channel coast if she cared to remember. Even in the drab Goutte d'Or women's eyes grew softer in expression as they put window-boxes outside their apartments and tied frail green stems to firmly rooted canes and sticks. The days grew longer. When the sun found its way through the skittish clouds rolling across the Seine it held the promise of warm days to come. Paris began to think of April and its magic of fresh green daubed on the trees.

However, before April arrived the Weber family would be in deep mourning.

At 1 bis Passage de la Goutte d'Or the first sun motes of spring were not golden drops to Jeanne Weber. She appeared sunk in deep melancholia, and her relatives of the Weber family glanced at the empty bottles when they called, then shrugged. Jeanne was not recovering easily, they decided, from the loss of her two first children. Had they known the little girl who had lived in the Breton fishing village of Keritry they might have found the abstract, withdrawn look on Jeanne's face sadly familiar. In their fashion they were brusquely kind, but they were practical-minded folk living hard hand-to-mouth lives, and they could not understand why a woman with a house to run, a husband and a child to feed, could not absorb herself in the task of daily living.

It was a blustery Thursday in that tragic March when Pierre Weber's wife knocked at the door of the end house in the narrow passage.

'Jeanne,' she said, 'I must go to the laundry, and I can't take Suzanne and Georgette with me. They're still recovering from pneumonia. Would you look after them?'

The laundry to which she referred was a public wash-house, where women from the poorer quarters with few conveniences at home took their family wash and scrubbed it.

'Yes, of course,' said Jeanne Weber. She put on her hat and

coat and the two women returned to the apartment Pierre Weber and his wife rented.

Suzanne was two months short of her third year and Georgette eighteen months. When their aunt sat down the smaller niece clambered on her lap, picking at a brooch she wore at her throat. The mother gathered up her large basket of washing.

'I'll get back as soon as I can, but you know what it is, Jeanne,' she said.

'I know,' her sister-in-law nodded. 'Take your time. Don't worry about the little ones.'

It was true, she did indeed know what washing clothes was like at the *lavoir* favoured by the children's mother. It had the romantic name of Les Deux Amis, but there was nothing romantic about the steam or the close smell of toiling women making mounds of lather with hard bars of cheap yellow soap as they fought a life-long battle with the grime that was the hallmark of their squalid living.

Some hours must pass before Pierre Weber's tired wife returned with the basket of clean wash to the small apartment. The woman blew a kiss to the children, smiled at Jeanne Weber, and the door closed after her.

Her steps faded on the wooden stairs.

In the event Pierre Weber's wife returned earlier than she expected to her home, her washing not half completed. She was scrubbing at the ribbed board in her tub when a hand clutched her arm. She turned to see the excited face of Madame Pouche, a neighbour, bent close so that her news could be heard above the noise of banging boards and chattering women.

'I knew you'd be here,' said the neighbour. 'You must go home at once, Madame Weber. I think something is wrong with Georgette. I heard her cry out as I was about to pass your place, and looked in. Your sister-in-law had Georgette on her lap and the poor little mite sounded as though she was choking.'

The alarmed mother abandoned her tub and pile of washing, rinsed her arms, and hurried back to her apartment with Madame Pouche. They found Jeanne Weber holding Georgette, and the aunt had one hand inside the child's clothes.

'I'm rubbing her,' she said. 'Something seems to be wrong with her breathing.'

She added that the child had gone blue in the face. The frightened mother took the little girl from her sister-in-law, massaged her chest, patted her back, held her to the open door to fill her lungs with relatively fresh air, and it seemed as though the child recovered. Suzanne, the elder child, stood by watching with wide eyes.

'She's all right now, Jeanne. Look after her,' said the mother, handing the child back to the aunt. 'I must go back and finish my wash.'

Again the dismal chore was interrupted, this time by her husband. Pierre Weber looked worried and his manner was urgent as he caught his wife's shoulder and spun her round.

'Look, come on home. Something's very wrong with Georgette. I think she's had a fit.'

When they entered their home it was to find their small daughter lying on the bed, her face wearing an unnatural dark tinge and her eyes appearing to protrude with a fixed unwinking stare. Georgette was dead.

There was a hurried consultation with Madame Pouche and Jeanne Weber. Someone was sent to summon a doctor. While the family waited, Madame Pouche took Pierre Weber on one side and said in a whisper: 'I don't like those bruises on Georgette's throat, monsieur. I think you should point them out to the doctor.'

The distracted man nodded agreement, but it is doubtful if the significance of the neighbour's remarks registered in his bemused mind. He did not point out the marks Madame Pouche's keen eyes had noticed to the busy doctor, who gave the dead child a cursory inspection, muttered his condolences, and wrote out a death certificate.

Cause of death was said to be convulsions. The date was March 2nd, 1905.

Nine days later Suzanne died in precisely similar circumstances, and, to judge by the death certificate issued by the same overworked doctor, for the same reason—convulsions.

On this occasion both parents had to be absent from home and could not take their daughter, so once more Aunt Jeanne was asked to come and baby-sit. The parents were not gone very long, but they returned home just in time to witness Suzanne's unpleasant death. Apparently the elder child also had a seizure or fit of some kind, for her face was contorted and dark in colour when the parents arrived back. The mother snatched up the child, whose mouth appeared wet with a thin foam, and unwound a scarf from around the throat. The scarf had been only lightly twisted, but again it was Madame Pouche who noticed the marks that looked like bruises on the flesh of the neck.

She pointed out the marks to the doctor. He nodded and started to make out the death certificate.

Suzanne joined her smaller sister in the local cemetery, and their tearful aunt was among the little group of mourners at the graveside. Indeed, Jeanne Weber appeared almost overcome by the tragic circumstances in which she had shared.

Two weeks later, on March 25th, she visited another of her sisters-in-law, the wife of Léon Weber, who suddenly recalled that she had to do some shopping before her husband returned home.

'Do keep an eye on Germaine while I slip out to the shops, Jeanne,' she said. 'I shall only be gone a few minutes.'

Germaine was seven months old and sleeping in her cot.

Léon Weber's wife had not walked very far from the block of flats where she lived when her mother, who occupied the flat above her, was alarmed by an infant's shrill cry coming from the home of her daughter.

Germaine's grandmother ran downstairs, burst into the flat of her daughter, and found Jeanne Weber with Germaine in her arms. The child was gasping for breath and losing her natural colour.

'Give her to me!' cried the grandmother, snatching the infant from its aunt.

The child was taken to the grandmother's apartment, where she recovered and was handed back to the mother when she returned from her shopping. Germaine was returned to her cot, and appeared to settle down comfortably. That was when the aunt remembered that she had some shopping to do. She asked her sister-in-law if she would go to the shops for her.

'My legs are bad,' she complained, 'and too much walking on them is painful.'

The mother, who genuinely liked Jeanne Weber, readily agreed to do the aunt's shopping. She put on her hat and coat again, picked up her shopping basket, and left.

She arrived back to find Jeanne Weber again holding a child that was having a fit. Her screams of alarm brought the grandmother and other neighbours hurrying to the apartment. A doctor was summoned, and when he left Germaine again appeared normal, and the puzzled man said he would call the next day. As soon as he had gone Jeanne Weber remembered something she had forgotten to ask her sister-in-law to buy for her.

'I'll slip out for you, Jeanne,' said the mother.

'It would be kind of you. My legs are so painful,' Jeanne Weber replied, appearing grateful for the other woman's kindness.

Incredible as it appears in print, the mother returned once again to find Germaine having one of those very mysterious convulsions. Jeanne Weber was bent over the child's cot and seemed to be bearing down heavily on little Germaine's chest. The frenzied mother had to tug hard at Jeanne Weber's arm to make her desist. She picked up her daughter and nursed her until her natural colour returned and she appeared to be breathing normally. Even then the mother was not suspicious of her sister-in-law. She went out with a neighbour to buy some salt and vinegar.

When she returned this time it was to find Jeanne Weber cradling a corpse in her arms.

'She had another of her strange turns,' said the tearful aunt.

On his second visit the doctor solved his puzzlement by proclaiming little Germaine had died of diphtheria. It was true that there was a diphtheria epidemic in Paris that spring, but Germaine Weber was not a victim of the virus.

Three days later Germaine was buried. The day was to be remembered with terrible clarity in the Weber family, for that night Marcel, Jeanne Weber's remaining child, who was seven, died of similar alleged convulsions.

He had slept with his mother.

Jeanne Weber herself was now the object of charitable pity. She was childless. She had lost her third child in precisely the same way as her sisters-in-law had lost their children. The family wondered if there could be a taint in their blood. It was not a pleasant thought if they had considered the fact that the only person present at all deaths was Jeanne Weber. But the simple truth did not occur to them, or if it did they were sufficiently dull-witted not to perceive its significance.

At last it was April. On the 5th the wives of Charles Weber and Léon Weber called on their sister-in-law in the Passage de la Goutte d'Or. The wife of Charles Weber brought her son Maurice, who was ten months old, to cheer his aunt from Brittany with his childish prattle. The three women shared a meal prepared by Jeanne Weber, who then complained that her legs seemed to be worse.

'I can't get about as I'd like to,' she told them, 'and I ought to go and get some needles. Of course, if Marcel had been here he would have gone for me.'

Mention of her dead son brought tears to his mother's eyes.

'I'll go for you,' offered Maurice's mother.

She went out, leaving her small son with his aunts. She had been gone only a few minutes when Jeanne Weber remembered she had to get some wine for her husband's supper.

Her sister-in-law made a joke about a poor memory and volunteered to go for the wine.

Maurice was alone with Jeanne Weber.

His mother returned to a horribly familiar sight to the women of the Weber family—Jeanne with a child in her arms who was apparently choking to death from convulsions. The wife of Charles Weber became savage in her swift resentment. Her tongue fashioned words whose import was realized only later.

'You miserable woman!' she exclaimed. 'He's choking to death while you look on—like the others did.'

She grabbed the infant from his aunt's arms.

Pierre Weber's wife went for a Dr. Mack, who arrived to find that Maurice was dead. The marks he found on the little boy's throat were, he decided, sufficiently serious to demand a post mortem. Two doctors, named Sévestre and Saillant, carried out the examination at a nearby hospital. They concluded that the child had died of strangulation. A police surgeon was consulted. He undertook a separate examination, and confirmed the finding of the others.

Jeanne Weber was arrested.

At once memories were jogged into startling disclosures. At least two other children had died in Jeanne Weber's arms from similar convulsions. They were two little sisters, named Poyatos, Marcelle, ten months old, and Lucie Alexandre, aged two years.

All Paris was gripped by a fever bred of hatred for the child strangler. To hatred was added confusion, for when the *juge d'instruction* appointed to examine Jeanne Weber's case, a Monsieur Leydet, in turn charged Professor Thoinot of the Paris Faculty of Medicine to examine the dead child, that worthy and eminent surgeon stated that he found no visible signs of strangulation and that in his considered opinion death was due to natural causes.

Monsieur Leydet was as startled as the rest of Paris. He ordered exhumations of the other bodies and further examinations by Professor Thoinot. The result was equally startling. The professor reported that he had found in the lungs of Georgette a swollen abscess and traces of the tuberculous bacilli Koch. In the neck of Suzanne he found a bruise caused while alive. The precise cause of death he was unable to provide, but he was convinced neither child had died from strangulation. This left Monsieur Leydet in an investigational vacuum, where he felt stifled. He asked for reports from two other medical men, Dr. Brouardel and Dr. Descouts. Before giving their opinions they cautiously consulted Professor Thoinot. Their official findings supported his.

The findings were printed in full in the national newspapers, and immediately an outcry arose. The public were incensed that medical science should appear to falter when asked to help bring justice to a child strangler.

On January 26th, 1906, Jeanne Weber first stepped into the court-room of the Seine Assizes to face a charge of multiple murder, while outside a mob chanted a refrain that had been sounding in Paris streets since the night before.

'Death to the ogress!'

The newspapers collected the name, and Jeanne Weber was indelibly stamped with it for all time. The mothers of Paris were bitter in their harsh denunciation of her. The mob clamoured for her head under the guillotine's axe.

Indeed, the only persons in the French capital not demanding retribution seemed to be the Weber family. They told reporters they thought Jeanne was insane and should not be executed.

'Better to put her in an asylum,' they urged.

They were very conscious of the stigma that would attach to the family if Jeanne Weber were executed.

Largely because the Weber family adopted this attitude towards the prisoner the police had two brain specialists, Dr. Wallon and Dr. Dupre, report on her. In a collective report they found her deportment calm and her speech lucid, but emphasized that she had apparently suffered from 'nervous upsets and hysteria as a result of mental disorders caused by the loss of her two children and certain gynaecological troubles'.

Jeanne Weber, in short, had her troubles like most women, but they had not affected her sanity.

During the trial the defence called three specialists to give evidence. They were the doctors Debuisson, Ségalas, and Joffroy, who stated that there was a marked history of alcoholism in the Weber family and that consequently children born of unions with members of the family were customarily of weak physical constitution and liable to suffer from convulsions.

The trial became a battle of medical experts.

Day after day Jeanne Weber remained calm and pale-faced, apparently listening to the rolling and ponderous phrases as though they were chords struck by an orchestra, with no true meaning for her. It is said her calm was shattered only after Germaine's mother denounced her forcibly and she turned and saw her husband, Marcel Weber, crying unashamedly in his seat.

Eighteen medical experts tried politely to call one another liars, and Maître Henri-Robert, defending the prisoner, made the most of the confusion they threw around like confetti.

When the amazed prisoner heard the verdict of not guilty she seized her counsel's hands and kissed them passionately. Maître Henri-Robert suddenly looked as concerned as though he had lost the case. The completely unexpected verdict brought a shocked and instantaneous change on the part of the public crowding the court and the streets outside. As the word of the acquittal sped from one section of the crowd to another the clamour died. The chant of 'Death to the ogress!' was silenced.

It was a case of emotional mass upheaval. When Jeanne Weber left the court she heard the crowd that had howled for her head now cheering her as though she were a heroine.

Time wrought another change. After the enthusiasm for the

acquittal had died rumours began to circulate. Life in Paris became a menace. She packed a bag and left the Goutte d'Or district.

For more than a year she was lost to the world that had been agitated by her trial. She took a number of domestic posts, and in April, 1907, she was housekeeper in the home of Monsieur Bavouzet, a widower who lived in Chambon. He had three children—Germaine and Louise, sisters, and their brother Auguste, who was seven. It was Louise who asked Dr. Papazoglou to come and attend her brother, who was sick and having convulsions. When the doctor entered the little boy's bedroom a hard-faced woman in dark clothes rose from a chair at the bedside. She said accusingly: 'Why didn't you come sooner? You might have saved him.'

Auguste was dead, but the body was garbed in a fresh nightgown. The woman said she had changed the boy's nightgown after he had passed away, as she termed his death. She also told the doctor that she was Madame Blaise, a sister of the children's mother. She said nothing about some strange bruises the doctor found on the dead boy's neck.

'I'm afraid I have no death certificate with me. I will send one round first thing in the morning,' Dr. Papazoglou told the hard-faced woman before taking his leave.

However, he took the precaution of reporting the strange neck marks to the authorities in Châteauroux. They sent their own medical man, Dr. Audiat, to examine the dead child. He made his examination on April 22nd and found numerous bruises not only on the boy's neck but also on the stomach, thighs, and forehead.

That was the day the dead boy's elder sister, Germaine, decided to explore Madame Blaise's room, where she found a magazine with an illustrated feature article on a woman referred to by the *Petit Journal*'s reporter as 'The Ogress of Paris'. The similarity with Madame Blaise could not be avoided, and the shocked and scared sister took the magazine to the local police.

Again Jeanne Weber was arrested.

Monsieur Belleau, the local *juge d'instruction*, had the same experience as Monsieur Leydet in Paris. The inquiry he conducted and the later court hearing was bedizened and bedevilled by conflicting medical evidence, and Maître Henri-Robert was there to help it along in his very professional way, which included inviting Professor Thoinot to climb on a band-wagon already overladen with medical experts. The fashionable and successful advocate had some valuable public relations service from a group styling itself grandiloquently the League for the Rights of Man, which held protest meetings, claiming that the woman held by the police was being persecuted. Monsieur Belleau was in an unenviable position. He scrambled out of it by sending Jeanne Weber to be tried by the Assize Court, where judges took one look at the muddled evidence, accepted Maître Henri-Robert's plea of 'judicial error', and discharged her, virtually without being tried.

It was Jeanne Weber's last hour of triumph. The journalists from Paris hailed her as something of a martyr. She was excellent copy, even though she made a poor photograph.

Shrewdly she changed her name and became Marie Lemoine, and found employment in a private sanatorium at Fontgombault. Monsieur Bougeau, a well-known philanthropist who ran the sanatorium for infirm children, had the kindly but mistaken thought that among children this unhappy woman who had lost her own would find companionship and a worthwhile purpose in her disordered life. She had been in the sanatorium only two weeks when an attendant found her standing with her hands around the throat of a small child. To avoid a terrible scandal, she was allowed to leave. Philanthropists are not immune from moral cowardice.

Jeanne Weber returned to Paris and called on Monsieur Hamard, the Chief of Police.

'I feel I must confess,' she told him, 'to the murders of my nieces and nephew. I strangled them.'

Monsieur Hamard was a man who knew cunning when he was confronted by it. He understood that the woman making this confession had been tried for the crimes she mentioned and been acquitted. She could not be tried again. But he knew that she had not been put in jeopardy of her life by the trial to determine whether she had murdered Auguste Bavouzet because the case had virtually been thrown out of court on her counsel's plea of judicial error.

'How about the Bavouzet boy?' Monsieur Hamard asked.

Her eyes blazed suddenly. 'I did not murder Auguste!' she cried, obviously aware of the importance of not confessing to this crime.

She was told to leave.

She eventually arrived in Saint-Rémy, near Toul, and lived with a workman named Emile Banchery. The pair journeyed to Commercy, put up at an inn, and the following day Banchery left her. The proprietors, a husband and wife named Poiret, had a little boy named Marcel. The visitor begged to have the boy share her bed for company. The inevitable happened. In the night a Madame Curlet, another guest at the inn, heard screaming, and rushed to the room from which the sounds came. She saw Jeanne Weber bending over the six-year-old Marcel, who had blood pouring from his gaping mouth. His face was turning black. Three bloodstained twisted handkerchiefs were draped over the bed. Into the room, in answer to Madame Curlet's cries, ran the landlord and his wife. Monsieur Poiret had great difficulty in dragging the frenzied murderess from the dead body of his small son. Then he saw the horror of what she had done.

Before strangling the child she had bitten out his tongue.

For the last time Jeanne Weber was arrested by the police.

Again she entered the now familiar court-room of the Seine Assize Court, and once more the medical experts began their controlled wrangling. This time over her sanity.

And again the chant went up in the streets outside the court, 'Death to the ogress!'

She was found guilty but insane and transferred to the asylum for the criminally insane at Mareville, where she was kept closely confined in a cell-like room fitted with iron bars. Her physical and mental condition deteriorated from the moment of her incarceration. She was found several times in the throes of a seizure, clutching at imaginary throats while she gasped for air. During these violent attacks she foamed at the mouth and wailed with terrible intensity.

One morning she was found stretched in death. She had her fingers securely locked around her own throat. The lust for death by strangling had finally destroyed her as she had destroyed her young victims.

8 * Daughter of Hatred

It was a broiling hot day in August when a seventy-year-old banker stopped and stared at an object glistening in the gutter. He stooped and picked it up. His find was a discarded cheap lock that had probably cost only a few cents. But the banker, like the general run of his kind, was a methodical man. An asset was an asset, and that was as true of a padlock as of a railroad or a steamship line. Moreover, his New England mind made him naturally careful with the little things of life. He was certainly careful with the cheap lock he had picked up. He took a small paper bag from his pocket, dropped the lock in, screwed up the bag, and returned it to his pocket.

Presumably satisfied with this acquisition of a fresh asset, he continued his ambling gait towards Second Street, where he lived with his second wife and the two daughters born to him by his first. He was a prosperous man but not a happy one.

And it was not only the heat that troubled him on August 4th, 1892. There was dissension in his home, and the atmosphere he breathed there was not conducive to relaxation.

He felt he had a right to be able to relax. He was a man who considered he had done his civic duty to the community in which he lived. He had for many years sold his fellow-citizens his patent burial casket, so that their departed loved ones would have their earthly remains preserved far longer than in any similar coffin. Or so he had claimed with the convincing firmness of a man who believes his own words.

In fact, he had made so much money with his coffins that he had obtained control of Fall River's four banks, and folks had come to think of him more as a banker than a mortician, which was soothing and gratifying when one reached the ripe age of Andrew Jackson Borden.

There was no thought in his mind that hot August day that within hours he would take permanent tenancy of one of his own desirable caskets, or that his demise would be bloody and violent. Much less that the circumstances attending it would provide the United States of America with a family murder mystery to occupy amateur and professional puzzlers with a tantalizing problem for generations to come.

A problem that would revolve around the name of Mr. Borden's younger daughter like a wheel around its hub. Her name was Lizzie Andrew Borden, and she was thirty-two, the same age as Mary Blandy had been when, exactly a hundred and forty years earlier, she had dangled, like a terrible black fruit, between two apple-trees in Oxford.

Women born in different worlds and in different ages, they were to rub shoulders in the annals of murder for the same crime—their fathers died unnatural and violent deaths.

Mr. Borden lived in a somewhat unprepossessing wooden house that was two storeys and an attic high. The neighbourhood was running down fast, for the industrial sprawl of Fall River was reaching out to engulf Second Street. Not that its owner cared, for appearances had never meant a great deal to him. Money was the rock on which he built his life. He had farm property which he visited from time to time when he could bring himself to make the trip. But seldom did he return to Fall River without a basket of fresh eggs to sell to the grocers in Main Street.

'A dollar is a dollar,' was one of his favourite sayings. Probably because the truth was incontestable. What he really meant was that a dollar was a dollar to him when it jingled in his capacious pocket.

His was a mentality that could perceive nothing incongruous in a man worth nearly half a million dollars stooping in the street to pick up a discarded lock. It was also the mentality of a man who did not fail to remember that his father had peddled fish through the coastal towns of New England. The occupation had proved not only smelly but highly precarious. In winter rough seas meant there was no supply of fresh fish. In summer hot suns meant folks didn't want the smell of cooking fish, even if it was fresh, in their stifling houses. Possibly because he was observant, and accustomed even when young to think for himself, Andrew Jackson Borden had chosen the profession of undertaker, aware that it had no seasons. Death was never out of fashion and no one could refuse to be buried.

However, although he had never shed the habit of wearing the sober uniform of an undertaker, he had certainly travelled a great distance in it. The man with the cheap lock in his little paper bag that August day was the president of the town's Union Savings Bank. He was a director of other banks, and a sizable stockholder in local woollen and cotton mills. His farms lay across the Taunton River.

He was approaching the gate in his front fence when he seemed to Mrs. Caroline Kelly, a neighbour, to cut her dead. She was on her way to the dentist's, but was so surprised at Mr. Borden's refusal to see her that she stopped and turned round to stare at him. She noticed that he looked very pale and tired. It crossed her mind that he might faint, and, as the wife of a doctor, she felt some responsibility towards an old man who might be suffering from the heat.

Mr. Borden went through his gate and reached the screen door at the side of the house. He tried to open it, but it must have been locked. He turned away and walked round the house to the front door. He was fumbling with his keys when the door was opened for him by the Bordens' Irish maid, Bridget Sullivan. Mrs. Kelly watched her neighbour disappear into his home, saw the door close on him, and turned to continue her way to the dentist's.

It was just after a quarter to eleven that hot morning when the Irish maid opened the front door to her master and Mrs. Kelly continued on her way down Second Street.

As Mr. Borden stepped into the hot gloom of the box-like house he heard something that genuinely startled him. It was the sound of deep-throated laughter, and it came from the landing above the steep staircase. He was startled because, as so many students of the circumstances surrounding his demise have pointed out, laughter rarely sounded in the Borden house. It was a home where hatred rather than the joy that begets laughter ruled the emotions of the inhabitants.

An ingrown hatred that thrived on itself, that was obscene because it was the very antithesis of family love.

Andrew Jackson Borden recognized the voice of the person laughing on the upstairs landing. It was his daughter Lizzie. If he thought anything about the sound it was probably that the temperature inside the house was too high for making such a disturbing racket.

Removing his hat, he walked into the dining-room, where there was a horsehair sofa that was not comfortable, but it was near the window, and he wanted to rest. He was seated on the sofa when Lizzie's step creaked on the lower stairs and a minute later she came into the room.

There was no sign of humour on her rather severe face, with its firm but full-lipped mouth, well-chiselled nose, and deep, somewhat small eyes set close together, so that when she looked at a person it was as though she was pointedly staring. Her hair was built tightly on to the top of her head in a low dome, and her full firm neck was touched by a narrow white ruff projecting over the collar of her closely waisted dark frock, with the row of small buttons running down the centre from throat to hem. Lizzie did not look younger than her years, nor did she look less strong-willed than events proved her.

She said, 'Is there any mail for me, Father?'

The man on the sofa shook his head. 'Where's Mrs. Borden?' he inquired in turn. It was customary in the household to refer to Mr. Borden's second wife as Mrs. Borden in a formal, unaffectionate way.

'She's out,' Lizzie told him. 'She received a note from somebody who was sick.'

Her father looked at her in surprise, but said nothing by way of comment on the information. He rarely mentioned his second wife to his younger daughter. Lizzie Borden had never forgiven him for remarrying. For a long time any mention by him of his second wife had been cause for a verbal explosion on Lizzie's part. Lizzie not only distrusted the short, dumpy, and excessively overweight Abby Durfee Gray Borden, who tipped the scales at more than fourteen stone, but she hated her abidingly because she feared that her father's wealth would be left to his second wife and not to his daughters. A natural corollary to this fear was that she and Emma might be left with nothing in approaching old age. Not altogether a groundless fear, because Emma was forty-one. The sisters must have frequently discussed the outlook for their future in the days when their father appeared to wilt in the summer heat. To them the prospect could not have appeared encouraging in view of the fact that the banker had given his wife's sister 'half a house' so that she would be assured of a home. The stepmother, it appeared, had sunk her wifely hooks not only into her husband but into his bank balance, and that concerned his daughters, Lizzie insisted. It was this insistence, carried to her father like open warfare, that had made life a burden for Andrew Jackson Borden, helped to send up his blood pressure, and filled the atmosphere of the wooden house with a steamy hatred.

Yet Lizzie was very much his own child, endowed with many of the characteristics of his nature, and although he apparently refused to recognize the fact, she certainly had his grasping acquisitiveness and readiness to dominate others. She had enjoyed no outlet for her instincts and proclivities other than teaching in Sunday school and certain duties in connection with the local Congregational church. She had once uprooted herself and joined a tourist group of spinster ladies on a trip to Europe, and for this reason enjoyed in her home town the reputation of being a travelled woman.

Emma's travels had been much closer to home. On that August day she was visiting some friends in Fairhaven, about fifteen miles distant, and was going on holiday with them. The only females in the house as Mr. Borden sat steaming on his dining-room sofa were the maid and Lizzie.

He picked up a copy of the *Providence Journal*, which had arrived by post, and started to read its news. Lizzie walked to the ironing-board she had set up in the dining-room, ran her hands over it, and without saying anything to her father went into the kitchen to collect a hot iron. She was about to iron some freshly washed handkerchiefs.

Bridget Sullivan entered with some wet cleaning cloths she had been wiping over the windows, on instructions from the absent Mrs. Borden.

Testing her iron, Lizzie said, 'Are you going out this afternoon, Maggie?'

The Borden sisters invariably called the Irish maid Maggie.

'I don't know, Miss Lizzie,' said the maid. 'I'm not feeling too well today.'

'Oh.' Lizzie Borden turned to look at her. 'Well, if you do go out, Maggie, be sure to lock the door. Mrs. Borden's out on a sick call, and I might go out myself.'

'And who's sick?' Bridget asked.

'I don't know,' Lizzie said. 'Mrs. Borden had a note this morning, so it must be in town.'

She continued by telling the maid that a dress shop in the town had a sale, but Bridget didn't appear very interested, possibly because she had no money to buy a dress, even in a summer sale. She repeated that she did not feel well, and said she would go up to her room and lie down. Her room was in the half-storey attic at the top of the wooden house.

The maid walked out of the kitchen and started up the stairs. It was eleven o'clock exactly, she said later, when she closed the door of her room, because she heard the church clock striking the hour. She also said she stretched out on the bed and closed her eyes. She dozed for from between ten and fifteen minutes, when she was startled awake by Lizzie Borden's shouting.

The maid jumped off the bed and opened her door, she said, and the words came clearly to her up the well of the staircase.

'Father's dead! Somebody came in and killed him!'

A truly shocking announcement that sped the Irish girl's feet down the stairs. She found Lizzie by the side-door, and turned to enter the sitting-room, to be stopped by Lizzie's sharp tone.

'Don't go in,' she ordered. 'I have got to have a doctor quick.'

Bridget ran out of the house and hastened to the home of Dr. Seabury W. Bowen, who for years had attended the Borden family, but he was still making his morning calls. Bridget asked the doctor's wife to be sure to send him to 92 Second Street as soon as he returned, and then hurried back to tell Lizzie, and ask her, 'Miss Lizzie, where were you when this happened?'

'Out in the yard,' Lizzie told her. 'I heard a groan and came in and the screen door was open.'

She dispatched the goggle-eyed Bridget to fetch Alice Russell, one of Lizzie's closest friends. Some minutes later another neighbour, a widow named Adelaide Churchill, saw Lizzie standing by the screen door, and from the look on Lizzie's face felt compelled to pause and inquire if anything was the matter.

'Do come over, Mrs. Churchill,' Lizzie called. 'Someone has killed Father!'

Aghast, the widow hurried to join Lizzie, who seemed to pull herself together.

'Where were you when it happened?' Mrs. Churchill inquired, repeating the maid's question.

This time Lizzie Borden answered differently. She said, 'I went to the barn to get a piece of iron.'

Later she was to change the piece of iron to lead sinkers or weights for her fishing-line.

Then Mrs. Churchill asked, 'Where's your mother?'

Lizzie had no liking for the second Mrs. Borden being referred to as her mother. She answered coldly: 'I don't know. She had a note to see someone who is sick, but I don't know but that she is killed too, for I thought I heard her come in.'

She caught her breath as she paused, and hurried on, 'Father must have an enemy, for we have all been sick, and we think the milk has been poisoned.'

Lizzie Borden, in short, was changing and enlarging her story at the same time. It was as though she was hurriedly improvising, suddenly anxious to disburse suggestions that would have to be considered later.

Mrs. Churchill was the first of a curious crowd of persons who invaded the Borden home before noon that day, all of them later to play their parts in a murder trial that was to make Lizzie Borden notorious. A policeman named George W. Allen examined the corpse of Mr. Borden and felt bile rising in his throat. The undertaker-banker was a frightening sight. His head had been hacked with a savagery that had destroyed his face and left one eyeball hanging from its socket. Constable Allen yelled, and ran from the house to warn his sergeant of what had happened. Dr. Bowen's firm medical stomach felt queasy when he surveyed the horror on the horsehair sofa, which was freely spattered with blood. The dead man's coat had been removed and he was wearing a cardigan. His legs had slipped from the sofa, and were in a spreading crimson pool.

'It sickened me to look upon the dead man's face,' Dr. Bowen stated later.

But he had a job to do. He examined the frightful head and counted eleven chopped cuts, some deep and nearly five inches in length. But the dead man's clothes were not disarranged, and his pockets had not been emptied, nor a ring removed from his hand. Dr. Bowen formed the impression that his old friend had been asleep when he had been struck the first murderous blow. He thought Andrew Jackson Borden had been dead less than twenty minutes when he examined him.

Bridget Sullivan had returned with Alice Russell by this time, and when the shocked medical man went into the kitchen he found them, with Mrs. Churchill, attending a collapsed Lizzie, one rubbing her hands, another loosening her frock, the third dabbing Cologne water on the forehead above the closed eyes.

But none of the three women so busy with Lizzie, or Dr. Bowen, who stood a little way off watching them, noticed any blood on Lizzie's skin or on her clothes. Lizzie opened her eyes, met the doctor's sharp stare, and quietly asked him to send a wire to her sister.

Dr. Bowen left to inform Emma that her father was dead. Lizzie watched him leave and asked one of the three women to go upstairs to look for her stepmother. The Irish maid seemed too scared to go alone, so Mrs. Churchill accompanied her.

They found Abby Borden in a room on the first floor, lying between a bureau and the bed. When Dr. Bowen returned from sending the wire to Emma he went up and saw that Abby Borden had been killed probably by the same hand and certainly in the same way as her husband, but in his opinion a full hour before. Her head had received a similar ferocious battering. She was lying face down in blood that was turning black. The death-dealing blade had snipped some of the hair from her head.

The horror of these brutal murders brought a stream of morbid neighbours to the house in Second Street, few of whom received the shock that was awaiting the Borden sisters' Uncle John. John Vinnicum Morse was their dead mother's brother and he was in Fall River on a visit to his brother-in-law and nieces. He had slept the previous night in the guest room where his late sister's successor as mistress of the house was found slaughtered. That bright sunny morning he had been out walking. He returned to the Borden home quite unaware that it was a house of death. He was looking forward to his midday meal, and for an appetizer wandered into the garden and picked some pears from a tree. He was well into his third when he walked into the house, sniffing to discover what was to be served. His appetite vanished when he stepped with both feet into the centre of a grisly tragedy in which he and his opinion would play their part. It is extremely unlikely that he finished eating the third pear, and reasonable to suppose that the two he had eaten sat very uncomfortably in his overturned stomach. He was something of a gourmet, but that August day almost cured him of gastronomic indulgence.

Long before John Morse received his next meal the police had arrived to begin questioning. What they were told covered that incredible half-hour from when Mrs. Kelly saw her neighbour enter his home by the front door to the awakening of the Irish maid by Lizzie's frantic calling.

What they perceived was that the double murder had been committed either by someone who had entered the house unseen and remained concealed or by a member of the Borden household. Granting, as Dr. Bowen believed, that the same person was responsible for both brutal slayings, then the only members of the Borden household who had been present and could have murdered Abby and Andrew Borden were Lizzie and the maid. When inquiry discounted the possibility of a phantom stranger hovering in the garden and leaping into the house to club to death the old banker and his wife, the choice hardened to one of Lizzie or Bridget?

It is still, more than seventy years later, the choice for anyone prepared to study the millions of words that have been written about the Fall River mystery.

The police acted, it would seem, very reasonably. They found a number of discrepancies in the evidence of persons who entered the Borden home shortly after the discovery of the bodies, but they did not rush to any conclusion before obtaining a few more significant facts.

For instance, they made inquiries about the note someone had allegedly sent the dead woman, according to her stepdaughter, who was known to hate her. They came upon no one who admitted sending such a note. Nor did they find anyone who had heard of such a note being written, except persons who had spoken to Lizzie.

Even more significant, they did not find the note.

A Fall River doctor named Handy told friends that he had seen someone whom he described as a 'wild man' moving suspiciously in the neighbourhood of the Borden residence around the time of the killings. The police went checking, and found that the person Dr. Handy had observed was a character well known to them for his ability to lower his own weight of rum. He was called Mike the Soldier. When he was located and questioned he readily agreed that he had been in the Second Street neighbourhood on the morning of the 4th. He also agreed that he might have had a wild look.

'I was getting over a long drunk,' he confessed.

On the Saturday after the murders the slaughtered parents were buried. It was estimated that four thousand citizens of Fall River crowded the streets along which the cortège passed on its way to the cemetery. Uncle John accompanied the bereaved sisters. Possibly due to his shepherding care they did not overhear some of the muttering among the crowd standing back from the graveside. But the rumours were reported to them that evening, and by a courier who appeared to feel it was incumbent on Lizzie Borden to remain indoors and not wander abroad. In fact, Dr. John W. Coughlin, mayor of Fall River, seemed uneasy about the direction in which suspicion was pointing, for not only citizens of Fall River were whispering that Lizzie Borden had struck the blows that killed her father and stepmother, but, as mayor, he knew that the police were thinking along the same lines.

The next day Lizzie was observed thrusting a dress into the stove in the kitchen. She insisted it was covered with paint. When this news reached the police they decided it could have been a bloodstained dress in which a murderess had committed a double murder.

By the time the inquest opened there were a good many questions to be answered by Lizzie Borden, who was emerging as the more forceful of the sisters, for Emma meekly did what Lizzie told her to do, and even stayed away from the inquest because that was the command she received from her younger sister. For three days Lizzie answered the questions flung at her by District Attorney Hosea M. Knowlton, who had arrived in Fall River on the Tuesday after the funeral and spent five hours in conference with Police Marshal Hilliard.

Knowlton's merciless questioning did not reduce Lizzie to tears, but it effectively removed many people's lingering doubts as to whether Bridget and even Uncle John could be involved. After Knowlton had finished he had Lizzie arrested on a charge of murdering her father. The warrant made no allusion to the murdered stepmother.

Once again a curious mass change of heart could be observed, one that might be said to have influenced the outcome of Lizzie's trial later. Under the leadership of certain church ministers some fairly resonant protests were made about the outrageous action of the authorities in arresting a well-known member of the Congregational church's flock. Some of them even called in person on the three judges appointed, according to the state laws of Massachusetts at that time, to hear the trial of the prisoner. There is no evidence that any of the judges so much as showed sympathy with the generous motives persuading their callers to make their most unwise and ill-considered visits.

The trial opened on June 5th, 1893, after ten months of legal manœuvring and manipulating. It was held in the New Bedford Courthouse. The benches allotted to the gentlemen of the Press were filled for the most part by reporters from the large American cities, for in the months since the murders the name of Lizzie Borden had rung across the North American continent like a clarion call.

Guilty or not guilty?

The outcome of the trial was hotly debated, and not surprisingly in Fall River partisan feeling rose to white-hot heat. The tide had turned in favour of Lizzie. Dark mutterings were heard about the Irish maid. The big-city reporters were more cynical. They were interested in the fact that if Lizzie was acquitted she would be a rich woman, sharing with Emma her father's sizable fortune. For since Abby Borden had died first, there could be no question of her having inherited from her dead husband.

The trial was a bitter affair. But it boiled down in one supreme essential to this. Lizzie could not have changed her dress and cleaned herself from butchering her father unless Bridget had been aware of what she was doing. The maid she always called Maggie insisted that she was up from her bed within fifteen minutes and saw nothing suspicious.

After fourteen days of parry and thrust by the opposed counsel Bridget's testimony stood, and, while it did so, to assume there was no reasonable doubt of Lizzie's innocence was clearly and manifestly impossible.

Even so, the jury, undoubtedly bemused by two weeks of giving close attention to repetitive detail, were absent from their seats for an hour and ten minutes, but when they returned it was to face a crowded and hushed court. Whatever their verdict, it would make history in the Commonwealth of Massachusetts.

'Lizzie Andrew Borden,' intoned the clerk of the court, 'hold up your right hand. Mr. Foreman, look upon the prisoner. Prisoner, look upon the foreman. What say you, Mr. Foreman?'

The foreman of the jury said two words instead of one.

'Not guilty.'

Lizzie Borden went back in the June sunshine to Fall River, and her procession was a triumph.

She was legally innocent. She was also an heiress. However, although she had her half-share of her father's estate, which left her with no further financial worries for the remainder of her life, she enjoyed little happiness. Her normally close relations with Emma were strained. The church folk who had so strongly and actively supported her now, upon her release, underwent a change of heart. They had heard a great deal of evidence at the trial, read scores of reports and theories, and with a good deal of what a later age came to call hindsight they came to a belated awareness that perhaps Lizzie Borden did, after all, commit the murders.

A piece of doggerel verse was circulating. It was full of errors, but it was an imposing although unpleasant jingle. It helped to make a good many partisan supporters of Lizzie change their allegiance. Those who knew her personally among the vacillating partisans also changed their attitude towards her. They gave her the cold shoulder, or perhaps it would be more truthful to say they tried. Lizzie did not give them much chance to succeed. She and Emma lived at Fall River through the immediate years following the trial, locking themselves up and seeing only a few friends. Bridget Sullivan was no longer their servant. With money given her by Lizzie she had gone to Ireland, where she is said to have bought a farm for her mother, and then returned to the United States under another name. She married, went west to Anaconda, in Montana, where she lived until 1948, when she died at the advanced age of eighty-one, well aware of that much-cited quatrain:

'Lizzie Borden took an axe
And gave her mother forty whacks;
When she saw what she had done,
She gave her father forty-one.'

That axe, the murder weapon, which would be more truthfully described as a hatchet, was never found in one piece. It had been washed of blood in the kitchen and removed to the cellar, where the handle was broken, possibly by a blow on a chopping-block, and the blade smeared with stove ash.

Only a very self-contained, grimly determined and deadly killer could have committed the double murder. The truth is that only Lizzie Borden herself had the qualities to support the character of such an axe murderess. She lived with Emma for a dozen years before the sisters became permanently estranged. By that time, 1905, Emma was in the middle fifties. She walked out on Lizzie, who had dominated her life, and did not return.

Neither of the sisters married.

Lizzie died on June 1st, 1927, and Emma on June 11th, ten days after. They came together for the last time in the cemetery at Fall River.

Both left most of their money to friends and relatives and societies for doing good works, including some which befriended animals. Among the private papers of the deceased sisters was found no letter or diary or journal with comments or notes to shed further light upon what is still termed the Fall River mystery.

But Lizzie's will contained one bequest that echoed faintly with the choked voice of the past—five hundred dollars for the 'care of my father's grave'.

The wraith of the old man who stooped in the August heat to pick up a discarded ten-cent lock must have been affronted at such a prodigal waste. Lizzie should have known better.

Well, perhaps she did. She left nothing for the care of her stepmother's grave.

9 * Siren of Doom

The Countess was anxious, and it showed in her lovely face. She had several times in a most exhilarating life known the proximity of violence, but it had never affected her as it did now.

This time she was unsure of herself. She knew that there were high stakes that could make the dangerous play truly deadly, and her anxiety increased until she felt afraid. It was not an entirely foreign feeling for the Countess Tarnowska, but it was one that had remained comfortably a stranger for a good while.

She became restive.

Half a million francs was a considerable fortune to most people in the first decade of the twentieth century. To the Countess it represented the difference between giving up her Venetian *palazzo* and keeping it, and with it her very comfortable way of life.

True, Venetian palaces were no longer in such high favour as in the heyday of Henry James, the American novelist who had for a time appeared obsessed by them as furniture for his fiction. But they were still symbols of aristocracy, even if not of financial status, for these were the years, shortly before the First World War, when Europe's aristocracy was entrenched in its social strongholds. It would take a revolutionary blizzard from the East and an economic drought from the West to change the climate so drastically that those social strongholds would become untenable except for the very few.

The Countess in her *palazzo* was a creature of doom, and she would not live to see the social changes in the dramatic years ahead. But she did not think of that as she waited for news from Donat Prilukoff, although violence coloured her thoughts, and she contemplated death as a solution to some pressing problems.

But not her own death.

She wanted to live. Passionately she wanted to live, and in the Adriatic sunshine she told herself she was happy, as happy as her dark Slav spirit could ever be.

Europe's Press had already told her story numerous times. Men had died for her beauty, it had been claimed, and a legend had grown up in the Venetian Russian colony about the daughter of the Eastern steppes whose loveliness was said to have made her lovers despair.

There was certainly a reckless streak in her, to counter-balance the dark undertones, and this she had inherited from a father descended from a line of Irish freebooters and sabre-wielding mercenaries. In her veins flowed blood that was a strange mixture of two civilizations, each steeped in its own inhibited passions that could enslave the heart and mind of man or woman.

In the Countess with the lovely figure and siren-like face those passions stirred their own dregs. For she was a creature of wilful impulses, self-indulgent, loving luxury, and withal hot-tempered when her will was crossed.

She was the daughter of Count O'Rourk.

More than two hundred years before Countess Tarnowska took up her abode in her *palazzo* overlooking the waters of a Venetian canal an Irish mercenary named O'Rourk sold his sword and allegiance to Peter the Great of Russia, when that empire-dreamer began building afresh in a backward continent he had inherited. This Irish soldier of fortune really gave meaning to the phrase. He helped Peter's military plans forward, by fighting for the Tsar and training new regiments to a fair degree of soldierly competence, and in return was given land, roubles, and a title.

A line of Count O'Rourks followed the founder of the family fortunes, and by the dawn of the century of Lenin and Trotsky they had established a veritable dynasty, and the Count O'Rourk owned estates not far from the Romanov capital of St. Petersburg. He also had a daughter named Maria. She was a dark-haired girl of strong will and even when quite young revealed an almost adult awareness of the sexual challenge presented by the proximity of a good-looking and physically attractive male. At the age of thirteen her father had her enrolled in a Kiev academy for the daughters of Russian nobles. For a couple of years she was instilled with the elementary lessons in general subjects required by young ladies of her class and the far from elementary lessons in deportment and social graces that were essential to that same rarefied stratum of the Russian social system.

She was not a bright scholar, but she acquired her full measure of deportment and social graces, together with not a few more personal allurements intended to embellish their eventual exercise. She had a pleasing voice, and musically her ear was true.

Anyway, there was no disagreement on this score by the cadets of the Tsar's training corps of officers in that Ukraine city at the junction of the Dneiper and the Desna. She was one of the stars in their off-duty firmament, and before she had entered her third year at the academy for young ladies she was the toast of barracks and the more select bars.

She was not sixteen when she returned to the north for a holiday and nonchalantly informed her frowning father that a prince and two counts were passionately and devotedly in love with his daughter Maria.

Count O'Rourk had been a young man himself. He had no reason to suppose young men had changed because he himself had lost his youth. He knew how easy it was for a young man to swear undying love and devotion to a girl who was flattered by such dramatic attentions, and he believed he also knew why the young man put on his most pleasing act. Usually because he hoped it would further his eventually attaining something he could not acquire by force without running foul of the law even in a country so feudally backward as the Romanovs' Russia.

So he had some inquiries made on his behalf. The information supplied to him from independent quarters assured him that the prince and one of the two counts would make admirable suitors for the young and impressionable daughter of the O'Rourks.

The second count was a very different proposition in any matrimonial sense. He was Count Vassili Tarnowska, and he came from a long and notorious line of wenchers and womanizers.

The young Maria was told to avoid this Vassili, who was the

most interesting male she had met up to that time. If it was experience that made him interesting, then she decided experience was no bad thing in a man. She found Vassili exciting to be with and she had no intention of obeying her father's wishes and avoiding him, or even of discouraging his most acceptable attentions.

She met him in secret, and such clandestine meetings added rare spice to the sense of adventure that prompted her to disobey her parent. Count Vassili Tarnowska was a young officer in the Tsar's Guards. His future was assured, and he could depend on receiving favour at Court, if he accepted the discipline and routine of his military status. But apparently what was a spice-laden sauce for the goose was equally exciting to the palate of a fashionable young gander. Maria disturbed Vassili's sleep. Being with her made all other women unnecessary in his little world. He wanted to marry her. He even stepped so far out of line as to tell her.

'Let us elope, Maria. It is the only sure way to happiness for you and me.'

It was romantic and thrilling, but even at seventeen Maria could keep her head on her shoulders when she decided it would be unwise to lose it.

'What of your career, my love?' she wanted to know.

'We shall be happy,' the impassioned young officer told her. 'Happiness will be our career.'

Heady stuff even for the head Maria was determined not to lose in a bright cloud of romance. After all, not every girl enjoyed a whirlwind elopement. It was an adventure that was straight out of a fashionable novel. Moreover, the fashionable novels always ended happily. They had to if they were to be fashionable, and Maria wanted to be fashionable, complete with happy ending.

It was as though a crazy logic convinced her head that what she felt in her heart was the right thing, that life with Vassili would be paradise on earth, and if she refused to share it she would always have regret.

So the young officer of the Tsar's Guards and the girl at the Kiev academy planned their elopement. Count Vassili Tarnowska shocked his superior officers by resigning his commission.

'You must be out of your mind,' his friends said.

'I am in love,' he retorted, as though it were reason enough for the most outlandish action.

His family were appalled when they heard the news. A son in the Tsar's Guards was a tradition sanctified by time and blood. They hated the daughter of Count O'Rourk, who they felt was responsible for bewitching their handsome Vassili and driving him out of his wits.

But the young couple were not staying to argue. They sped on a honeymoon before slaking their enthusiasm by getting married. Nothing that occurred on the honeymoon created need to revise their high opinions of themselves or each other. Ahead stretched a life brimming with bliss. Such bliss, however, could not be risked by an irregularity that was utterly unconventional. So they duly appeared before a bearded priest and side by side sank on their knees and had the holy man poise a crown over their heads to make them husband and wife according to the ritual of the Russian Orthodox Church.

Then the interrupted honeymoon was continued. It was of far greater duration than any conventional honeymoon, but the young couple had a great deal of mutual passion to slake, and their Slav resources for creating more seemed truly unending. However, two years later they were back in Kiev of pleasant memories, the parents of two children of whom their mother was not overfond. Indeed, she found the restrictions and trammels of motherhood an unnecessary price imposed by a Mother Nature who appeared to lack any real sense of discrimination. She refused to consider she should become the brood mare for her stallion-like Vassili. Not unnaturally a coldness crept into the intimacies enjoyed by husband and wife, and those intimacies lost not only their savour but their tender appeal. Count Tarnowska began to look in other directions, and was not long in finding other eyes that sparkled when they met his.

Soon he found compensations away from home for the pleasures he felt were being denied him.

However, Tarnowska was an intensely jealous man. Jealous of his family name, his manhood, his reputation, and what he considered his honour, which in actual fact was a consideration limited to his wife's behaviour.

Many looked at the siren face of the Countess and felt a stirring in their blood, especially when she held their gaze and smiled back at them. But all save one remembered that Tarnowska, who had been in the Tsar's Guards, was an expert and noted swordsman and that he had a quick temper and the strength of a bull when angry. So the Countess's bright glances made many male hearts flutter but won her no secret adventures.

The exception was Vassili's younger brother Peter. It was in a spirit of revenge for her husband's extra-marital excursions that the Countess set herself to seduce the comparatively inexperienced Peter. He was easily embroiled in a secret affair from which he could not extricate himself without loathing his folly and despising himself. In a fit of grim remorse he returned to his father's home and hanged himself.

The Countess was rewarded when she saw how the news of the tragedy affected her husband. She experienced a deep sadistic joy. She took down her journal, kept to remind her of the delights of love in her later years, and read:

> 'I was seventeen and wise beyond my years. But, sagacious as I thought myself, I could not believe anything against Vassili. My eyes saw nothing but him. On the 12th of April I ran away with him. We were married in a little church on the desolate steppes. I never thought life could hold such joy.'

But now that fine spring fever was over and she saw with the eyes of experience the clay in the average man's human make-up. She felt she could grasp it and shape it to her own desires. When she looked at Alexis Bozevsky, an Imperial Guards officer, she was sure. Which was a very warming sensation. For Bozevsky had the reputation, whether deserved or not, of being the most handsome man in Russia. Bozevsky, moreover, was no stripling. When a woman looked at him he understood what was meant by her gaze. When Maria Tarnowska gave him her fluttering glance he responded. He was invited to a banquet given by Tarnowska. Because he was popular with the women and a noted ladies' man he was asked to propose the conventionally laudatory toast to his lovely hostess. He went rather far in his lyrical fashion, but because he was as noted for his open audacity as for his cavalier practices he got away with it at the table and was applauded for this piece of inflated lyricism:

'To those red lips which I have kissed
I raise this glass of wine;
I bless the radiant loveliness
That made my life divine;
And bless the hour that brings me death,
For the hour that thou wert mine.'

However, Tarnowska had second thoughts about that extravagant tribute when he left the banquet table, and decided to prove that his guest was an unsuspected prophet. Later, in the early hours of the morning, he appeared with a pistol in his hand while Bozevsky was settling down in his troika and preparing for a fast gallop back to his lodging. For an erstwhile officer Tarnowska the noted swordsman was a poor shot. His bullet caught Bozevsky in the back of the neck but did not kill him. Tarnowska gave himself up to the police, while his tearful wife hovered round the doctor summoned to attend the wounded Bozevsky.

Bozevsky lingered for three months, nursed by Maria, and when he died the now notorious Countess Tarnowska was fluttering her dark eyes at a lawyer named Prilukoff, who was a married man with a family, which did not prevent him feeling the siren's seductive allure or responding to it as no married man should allow himself, especially one fortified by legal tenets and training. But possibly because he had his legal training to fortify his acceptance of his own surrender to the lovely Countess, Prilukoff eventually saw how his relationship with the siren could be turned to an advantage that might be counted in roubles.

He was known to Count Paul Kamarowsky, who was old enough to be the Countess's father, but who had earned the reputation of a connoisseur of beautiful women. Indeed, on the subject of feminine allure and loveliness Count Paul was thoroughly convinced he spoke with the voice of authority. When he saw Countess Maria Tarnowska it was as though his recent crowding years fell from him. He was a young man again, fired with enthusiasm and desire.

The Countess did her best to help him foster the illusion.

So did the Scorpion, as she had cruelly dubbed Donat Prilukoff when she tired of his physical expressions of affection, and when his financial help after Bozevsky's death was exhausted.

Count Kamarowsky had made the Grand Tour in his youth, and he recalled the sunshine and delights of other lands. He now decided he could enjoy them again in later life, and perhaps more fully, in the company of the lovely Maria. She evinced no lack of enthusiasm for seeing the world beyond the Russian frontier, and arrangements were made for a journey to the south of Europe.

Maria Tarnowska saw the Riviera, the Austrian Tyrol, and northern Italy in the company of her ageing lover. Her vivid pleasure at the new sights and experiences heartened Kamarowsky to dally. He took his lovely siren to Venice and she was wafted along the Grand Canal by moonlight to the singing of gondoliers.

These were the most romantic days of her mature life. But she had not lost her ability to weigh the pros and cons of living and to decide what was best, in her opinion, for Maria O'Rourk, the girl of mixed blood and strong desires.

She wrote in her journal:

> 'Prilukoff still held me bound to him by the bond of gratitude. But Count Kamarowsky was swaying me towards a brighter and securer future. My marriage with Vassili, so long merely an empty and nominal tie, was about to be dissolved by a decree from the Holy Synod, and Kamarowsky implored me to marry him. His sadness and the loneliness of his little son moved me deeply. The thought of bringing light and joy into their lives was unspeakably sweet to me, while for my part I rejoiced to think that by the side of a worthy and honourable man I might take my place in the world once more, rehabilitated and redeemed.'

Savouring that literary meringue more than fifty years after it was penned, one cannot avoid the cynical reflection that it was intended to create a false impression in the reader. If not, then the writer was merely striking an attitude to amuse herself, for the picture of the woman desirous of bringing joy into the lives of an elderly man who was her lover and of his small son is touching, but utterly at variance with her past record. Already Peter Tarnowska and Alexis Bozevsky had paid with their lives for their dalliance and submission to her sexual appeal. She could have changed, for everything is possible. But balanced against the facts of what the future held after she wrote those words it is extremely unlikely.

Donat Prilukoff, who not only seemed perpetually mesmerized by her physical charm, but was well aware that the introduction to Count Kamarowsky had still to be exploited in a way that would prove compensatory for his professional services and advice, arrived to smile his cynical appreciation of how the liaison was developing.

To Countess Tarnowska he came as a shadow to darken her days if her journal can be believed at all.

Again she wrote:

> 'A great fear clutched me and I asked him, "Are you cross with me?"
>
> "Cross?" he shouted, leaping to his feet, his eyes glaring like those of a madman. "Cross? No, I am not cross." I recoiled from him in terror, but he followed me, pushing his distorted face close to mine. "You ruin a man, you drive him to perdition, and then you inquire whether he's cross. You take an honourable man in your little talons and turn and twist him around your fingers. You mould him and transform him into a thief. Then you throw him aside like a dirty rag and you ask him if he's cross!"
>
> I burst into tears. "Why—why do you say that?" I sobbed.
>
> "Why do I say that?" stormed Prilukoff. "Why? Because I had a wife and I betrayed her for you. I had two children and I forsook them for you. I had a career and I lost it for you. I was a man of honour and I turned thief for you." '

This passage from her secret journal is a complete revelation. She would never have written it had she not enjoyed the vicarious thrill from recounting the incident. Possibly it didn't occur precisely as she related. But here in essence is the agonizing drama of a man she had defeated and used—and, moreover, was determined to use again if Prilukoff could come up with a scheme that was worth carrying out.

And he could. Whether he felt the way his words in the journal suggested is not very material. He was there, away from Russia and his family, dancing attendance on the woman whose life he had entered at a potentially dangerous time for her, when her husband feared he might be sent to Siberia for shooting Bozevsky, a dismal event that did not transpire. A time when she had come as close to panic as Maria Tarnowska ever allowed herself to, for she understood that failure to face up to the consequences of one's own actions was merely surrender for the worst of all reasons.

But as she stood in her *palazzo* awaiting Prilukoff she knew she had to be rid of the incubus of Kamarowsky and possessed of such money as his death might bring her. Half a million francs.

And everything depended on Nicholas Naumov, another young man who was in love with Maria Tarnowska because his eyes were enchanted by what he beheld when she smiled at him. Naumov was the son of the Governor of Orel. He was also a friend of Kamarowsky.

But first Prilukoff had to succeed in his lawyer's mission.

When he arrived at the *palazzo* the Countess was calm, but she had to probe, for the lawyer could mask his feelings, and she knew he enjoyed tantalizing her. It was his one way of reaching her and making her feel he remained in her life.

So he took his time, but she learned soon enough that the scheme they had worked out from one of Prilukoff's ideas was going to work. First the lawyer had compiled a letter to the Countess allegedly from Prince Ivan Troubetzkoi, offering marriage and, as proof of his devotion to the woman he looked upon as a goddess, a readiness to insure his life for half a million francs, naming her as sole beneficiary—when she was his wife.

Maria had only seen Prince Ivan once in her life, and had probably never spoken to him.

The bogus marriage proposal was shown by Prilukoff to Kamarowsky, the lawyer pretending to be doing the Count a considerable favour. Suddenly afraid that he would lose the lovely woman he had brought from Russia, Kamarowsky readily, when helped by suggestions from the wily lawyer, drafted a will in favour of the Countess, making her the beneficiary of an insurance on his life for half a million francs.

'He is at this very moment putting through the insurance details, my dear Maria,' Prilukoff told her, smiling in triumph. 'So I have done well, wouldn't you say?'

'Excellently, my dear Donat. And now?'

'Now you make sure Naumov does not fail us. Now, Maria, it is up to you.'

With exquisite competence the Countess Maria Tarnowska prepared to play the most demanding seduction scene of her life as a siren luring men to folly and doom. She met Nicholas Naumov by secret arrangement stage-managed by Prilukoff. There were very soon large tears welling in the dark violet eyes, and the young man found it impossible to refuse the role of her protector. He demanded to know why she could not keep from tears when she should be happy, and in a broken voice she told him that Kamarowsky was a sadistic monster destroying her life with his brutal demands on her. She saw no way ever of escaping him.

It was an inflammatory performance. Young Nicholas Naumov took her in his arms, and the tear-stained face was upturned to his. He smothered it with kisses.

'I shall free you from him,' he promised.

'Will you?' she murmured, with just a tinge of doubt in her voice to release more rash promises.

She did not ask how this promised freedom would be achieved. She had no wish to be involved. In fact, the plot was designed to leave her isolated from any violence she had released. When events had taken the only course they could in the explosive atmosphere she was creating she wanted to appear as a wronged woman, a helpless female over whom men wrangled because they were unable to withstand their own desires.

Countess Maria Tarnowska was playing a deadly role, but one known since the days of Delilah. She had her own modern improvements and enlargements for the classic theme of female seduction. Two men should be destroyed, and from the wreckage of their lives she should collect half a million francs. As an actress she was determined to be well rewarded for her performance. Just what Donat Prilukoff, her willing and urbane stage manager, would net for his professional services is an item she did not commit to her journal.

But she was content that she had played her part well when she escaped at last from Naumov's possessive arms. The liaison with Kamarowsky had served her most usefully, had brought her across Europe to a way of life she had no intention of willingly forsaking. But it was as good as over by the time she reached her *palazzo*.

That parting from Naumov had been, on her part, all tenderness and gratitude, a climax of underplayed emotional gratitude, so different from earlier sessions when the young man of tempestuous declarations had allowed her to crush out her cigarettes against his bare flesh. Or on that memorable occasion when her sadism had produced a masochistic frenzy in him as she carved her initials in the flesh of his arm before rubbing astringent toilet water into the cuts. These were some of her Delilah antics the young fool cherished and in his blind conceit made her his living destiny.

Nicholas Naumov called on his older friend Count Paul Kamarowsky, and was greeted by a smile and open arms. Rather pale, and obviously tense, Naumov produced a pistol from his pocket and levelled it at Kamarowsky.

'For Maria,' he said fiercely.

He emptied the gun. Its five bullets ended the plot and kept a promise.

Kamarowsky had been removed from Maria Tarnowska's life.

The murder became a sensational *cause célèbre*. Police and magistrates, reporters and friends of the dead man, doctor and prosecutors—all had plenty to say. Only one person remained silent in the noisy furore the murder had released. That was Maria.

'Don't say a word,' had been the advice of her lawyers.

It was good advice, and she took it.

She became headlined as the 'Sphinx in Crêpe' and the 'Siren of the Adriatic' in newspapers as far from Venice as South America.

Because so many tongues wagged in Venice the plot was uncovered. Instead of a *crime passionnel* the brutal contriving to use a foolish tool to secure half a million francs was held up to the public gaze as a sordid intrigue for gain.

Prilukoff emerged as the arch-villain of the piece, Naumov the hot-headed and arrogant assassin who wanted what his friend considered his.

The siren of doom remained something of an enigma. Her silence was two-edged. It allowed some, including her detractors, to assume the worst. It allowed others, especially the more romantic-minded of reporters and newspaper readers, to believe her an unfortunate woman destroyed by a beauty desired by men who refused to leave her alone.

The French writers alluded to *beauté du diable*. It was a high-flown phrase not rooted in stern realism, but it came very close to the essential truth. Countess Maria Tarnowska's beauty had certainly produced more devilish results than goodly.

When she, with Donat Prilukoff and Nicholas Naumov, appeared before the Venetian court they had no less than twenty-seven charges to answer. Throughout the entire battle on the courtroom floor it was the siren in mourning who held the eyes of spectators. She looked pathetic, demure, even wronged. Had she spoken she might have cleared up some misunderstandings. But she remained an enigma in crêpe, causing counsel to perspire, but giving them no opportunity to do more than wrangle over her, as males had been doing ever since she arrived at the Kiev academy for young ladies. The jury had to do some wrangling, too, and took their time over it. After their findings had been presented, the judges held a conference, and the court's president announced their decisions.

Prilukoff to go to penal servitude for ten years, Naumov for three, the silent siren for eight.

So in 1910, that same year when the Paris mob shouted 'Death to the ogress!' for the second time in Jeanne Weber's life, a woman of very different social class and upbringing, but just as deadly in her fashion, was sent to an Italian prison. The harsh reality she had to accept almost killed her. Her mental and physical health became so impaired in prison that the Italian authorities released her some time before the completion of her sentence. She changed her name, became for a time a nurse in a military hospital, and died shortly after the First World War.

10 * Blows and Bullets with Love

Fifty-three years separate the murderous performances of two British women who would have been acquitted by French juries. Both were driven to murder by minds made frantic and distraught through the collapse of their love-lives. They killed their lovers because those lovers were no longer theirs. What they had lost they would not surrender readily. What they could no longer possess they would destroy.

These are among the most powerful reasons for women becoming deadly.

Separated in time by more than half a century, Kitty Byron and Ruth Ellis were veritable twins in tragedy. Making allowances for the different periods in which they lived, the firm lines of similarity are truly striking in so far as they reveal the character that looked in upon itself and found the perverse courage to slay in the open street.

Both gave of themselves freely. Both could not face loneliness after love. Both refused to accept reality as applying to her. Both killed their lovers in London.

Reginald Arthur Baker was a stockbroker with an eye for a pretty ankle and a pretty face. Pretty ankles were about all the man in the street saw in the first years of the present century, for skirts were long and veils were fashionable. Baker liked women, their company, their chatter, the fact that they flattered him for merely being a male, and as an ardent pursuer of pretty ankles he had some advantage in the fact that his pockets were well lined. As a stockbroker, he mixed with men of calculated and sophisticated tastes.

When he first saw Kitty Byron he was like an eight-point stag perceiving a new hind in the forest. He swept her off her feet in a fast and very furious courtship. One that was thrilling to both of them.

Kitty Byron was a pretty girl. She had an hour-glass figure, looked like one of George Edwardes's Gaiety Girls, and she massaged Baker's male ego with her very femininity. He decided he was in love.

She knew she was.

She was the kind of young woman who could even be in love with love, because Reginald Baker was a person quite new in her limited experience. He made a dashing figure of a man with the enchantment of City sovereigns gilding him in Kitty's eyes. She saw that she could be happy only with him. He told her how happy she made him.

She had scruples, but he overcame them with ardent wooing and even more ardent promises. He painted a pretty picture of life together, even anticipating her girlish dreams. In only one particular was he purposefully reticent. He refused to discuss marriage.

Which shows that Reginald Baker, for all his fine talk as a lover, was more cautious than the girl he wanted to live with him as his wife. But while Kitty Byron was desirous of matrimony, she settled for a home with a maid and no benefit of clergy. After all, she consoled herself, the man she loved must come to realize, given time, that he could not live without her any more than she could without him.

A very natural form of human equation in which a great many love-blind persons indulge. But it has no counterpart in mathematics, where two and two can only make four and love is not even an unknown quantity. It doesn't exist.

Possibly had Kitty Byron been a little more worldly-wise, had she been able to add two and two correctly, she might not have allowed her trim ankles to be swept up the deep-carpeted stairs to the comfortable flat which she was allowed to consider her home.

But having arrived there, having cut her emotional painter and allowed herself to drift, she set herself to enjoy the drifting. And to Baker's credit it must be admitted he made it a most enjoyable sensation. Life became, in practice, only very little short of a truly matrimonial round of pleasure-filled hours. The one thing missing was the conventional strip of gold around her third finger left hand, but as that finger was decorated with a band of the same metal on which a cluster of gems glowed she could fool herself with fancies just as pretty.

To keep her mind from dwelling on the one major shortcoming in her life she was taken to frequent cosy supper parties after an evening at the theatre. There were week-end trips to the country, shopping excursions, visits to the parks. It was all very idyllic in a London with sobering news from South Africa and fluctuating prices on the Stock Exchange.

Not that Baker brought any day-to-day City problems to the love-nest he shared with his adorable Kitty, as he called her. But some of the gilt inevitably became rubbed off the ginger-bread existence. The novelty was lacking on occasions when the couple tried to recapture a lost ecstasy. To the woman, revelling in possession, this was only a temporary phase, one to be discounted in favour of all the future held. To the man it was a sign that he was getting used to what he had. Maybe another pair of trim ankles was the solution. It had been in the past.

He found occasions to stay away from the flat. He made excuses, and some of them sounded laboured even in his own ears. He also revealed a hidden talent for reaching the bottom of a bottle in very short time.

The rift was very noticeable in the lute.

The love-nest resounded to the foreign noises of voices lifted in anger, and after the first quarrel Kitty Byron sobbed as though her heart was broken. The quarrel was patched with kisses and renewed tenderness, but patchwork is never like the untorn fabric. The mend shows. The patch can even become an eyesore if one has little liking for it and is not strong-willed enough to ignore it.

Kitty Byron was not strong-willed.

She adopted a typical feminine tactic towards the male who had sharply disappointed her and caused her to endure some tearful and sleepless nights. She gave him what in that day was known, not very politely, as the length of her tongue.

Baker's reaction was sharp and stinging.

'Why don't you stop nagging?' he shouted. 'You're not my wife.'

It was like a blow from a knotted fist. The reminder of her

insecure status in his life stung like acid on raw flesh. She felt bruised and scalded. This time Baker was impervious to her tears.

'We might as well face it,' he said sullenly. 'This little affair is over.'

He felt differently after being away from Kitty for a few days. But even she understood that things were not the same when he came back. The fire they had lit had gone out. It could not be long before the embers chilled.

She did nothing and said nothing to annoy him. She lived daily in a torment of emotional indecision, suspended between anguish and hope. It never occurred to her that she was romanticizing the commonplace.

It was otherwise with Baker the stockbroker and man of the world. Kitty Byron's stock had drifted rather low. It had happened before with other women. It would happen again in the future. He was ready to get out, cut his loss—if an unwanted mistress could be considered a loss. He must have resolved any doubts on the subject because when his mind was made up he packed his things and informed Kitty tersely: 'I'm leaving you. I should have done it weeks ago.'

The rent, in short, was beyond patching.

'No, Reggie,' insisted a frightened woman striving desperately not to throw hysterics. 'You can't leave me. I won't let you.'

To the man whose mind was made up it sounded farcical.

'I don't see how the hell you can stop me,' he said, with none of his erstwhile chivalry shining about him like polished armour.

'I can kill you,' she said quietly.

Reginald Arthur Baker made the mistake of appearing amused by what he considered the empty words of a disappointed and dejected woman who couldn't bring herself to admit the truth.

'Talk sense, Kitty,' he said. 'The world's full of men and it's full of women too.'

The rent on the flat was paid up. He took his bags down to a hansom cab, came back for his coat and hat. On the way out of Kitty Byron's life he displayed another streak of cruelty. He cracked a coarse joke with the maid. Then he returned to the cab and jog-trotted to his club.

The maid, herself a little scared and very concerned about her own immediate future, crept into the room where Kitty Byron stood staring into space.

'What are you going to do now, ma'am?' she inquired.

'I'm going to kill him.'

Like Reginald Baker, the maid thought she was listening to a distracted woman's empty threat after her personal world had crumpled around her. She was to change her mind when Baker was no longer able to change his.

Baker had escaped to a gay bachelor week-end. Kitty remained a prisoner in the flat, confined with her thoughts. Hourly her mood became more desolate, her thinking more desperate. When the week-end was over she had changed without realizing the significance of the change. She had crystallized her despair into two alternatives.

Reggie would come back to her or she would kill him.

In the dragging hours of that lonely week-end she had self-induced a traumatic state of mind and achieved a degree of mental derangement which, while it did not impair her reason, certainly stimulated her to take the course she followed. It was temporary and could not last. But while it lasted she was not entirely responsible for the thoughts that prompted and governed her actions.

On the Monday morning after the lonely week-end her first significant act was to dress herself with extra care. She left the flat and walked to Oxford Street. She entered a shop and said to a salesman, 'I want to buy a knife.'

He sold her a clasp-knife that was not designed for use by the kind of hands she possessed. She had considerable difficulty in prising up the stiff, bright new blade. But the point was sharp and the edge keen and she was satisfied with her purchase, feeling it would serve well the purpose for which she had bought it.

She was right. It did.

From Oxford Street she made her way to the City. In an entire year she could not have chosen a worse day for her intention. The streets were jammed with Londoners out to see the Lord Mayor's Show. She reached the post office in Lombard Street, went inside, and wrote a note to Baker. She found a messenger, gave him the note, and told him where to deliver it.

It was one o'clock.

An hour later the messenger returned wearing a look of apology.

'I'm sorry, lady, but when I found him,' the messenger reported, 'he said I was to tell you he couldn't come.'

Baker was evading her, as she had more than half suspected, which was why she had written a second note. She handed it to the messenger and told him to return with it to Baker.

This note shook its recipient. In it Kitty Byron said she was determined to see him, but she omitted to say why. If Baker had been shrewd he might have wondered at that. She continued with what was virtually a threat. If he did not come to her at the Lombard Street post office she would come to the Stock Exchange and force her way inside. Baker was alarmed. Such an attempted female invasion of that citadel of males and money could only result in a scene which would be reported in the halfpenny Press. It would be a scandal, something he had to avoid even at the cost of going to the Lombard Street post office and facing another round of villification and tears.

Kitty Byron saw him come scowling into the post office where she had been waiting until her legs had grown numb.

'I've told you,' he began heatedly, 'I don't ever want to see you again. Now stop this nonsense and let me get back to the Stock Exchange and don't annoy me any more.'

'Reggie, you can't leave me.'

The final plea fell on deaf ears. Baker had sidestepped scandal in the Stock Exchange, but he had no intention of allowing her to create a scene in the post office. He turned and hurried out into Lombard Street, at that time crowded with sightseers returning from watching the Lord Mayor's Show. The numbness left Kitty Byron's legs. She hurried after him, fumbling at her handbag. Baker was not far past the post office, pushing through the press of people, when the clasp-knife's blade ripped into his body. Several times the infuriated young woman with the glazed eyes struck at the tottering man. Horrified passers-by grabbed the seemingly demented woman, and held her while Baker stumbled to a wall, tried to hug it to him, and slowly slid down it. He was bleeding profusely.

The glazed look left Kitty Byron's eyes. She tore loose from those holding her back and reached Baker to bend over him, then fell on her knees beside him. She began kissing his pale face with terrible passion, cradling his blood-smeared upper body in her arms.

When the police pulled her away Baker was dead.

The murder roused all Britain with a mixture of compassion and horror. It is said hundreds of men wrote to Kitty while awaiting trial, many offering marriage. Some of the marriage offers were wired.

She was tried at the Old Bailey before Mr. Justice Darling, but the law the learned judge had to administer that day in 1902 provided no room for the admission of extenuating circumstances, and the summing-up left the jury in no doubt as to their duty. Kitty Byron was found guilty, with a recommendation to mercy which the judge could only ignore, and Mr. Justice Darling sentenced her to death.

Awaiting death, she received even more fantastic offers, this time from a number of men who professed to be ready to die on the gallows in her stead.

The majority of people in Britain, while not condoning Kitty Byron's peculiar morals in that late Victorian era, nevertheless felt life had dealt with her harshly. She had loved too ardently, too possessively.

A few days before she was due to meet the hangman in Holloway Prison the Home Secretary, bowing as much to public clamour as to that formal recommendation to mercy by the jury, commuted her death sentence to one of imprisonment for life.

The human parallel to Kitty Byron ended outside the Magdala public house in Hampstead on Easter Sunday 1955 when Ruth Ellis came to the end of her own emotional road and shot dead David Moffett Drummond Blakely after loving him as intensely as a Klieg light radiates actinic rays.

She too had been the mistress of the man she killed. She too had pleaded for his return when the rapture had evaporated with that same fine carelessness with which it had been engendered. She too sought alternatives and found only death to be acceptable.

However, the parallel between the two women killers has a few intermittent points of divergence before extending to the ultimate tragedy.

Ruth Ellis had been born Ruth Neilson in the Welsh seaside town of Rhyl, a child of a Belgian mother and a musician. Her most formative years were those while bombs were dropping on London and other towns. She was a café waitress at fourteen, and when she had the fare she came to London, where she met an easy-smiling French Canadian who was a married man, only that was something about himself he did not tell the fair-haired girl with the wide bright eyes whom he accepted as a stand-in for the woman somewhere in Canada.

Ruth Neilson matured fast. Early motherhood ensured that. She found herself facing the necessity of providing for herself and her infant son. She caught some of the first post-war frenzy when she worked long hours and late at a number of clubs as a hostess to men in civvies getting rid of their Service gratuities. In one club she met a dentist who liked her looks and her smile enough to ask her to marry him, so that he could enjoy them permanently.

Ruth Neilson became Ruth Ellis in Tonbridge, and later the dentist became the father of a daughter.

The marriage did not last, and because it failed her she considered herself disillusioned. In this mood of regretfulness she returned to the world of bright lights behind heavy shades and subdued whispers in lonely corners. She was back where she felt she belonged, where the barman could reach for her favourite Pernod and where the well-groomed wolves with well-lined wallets could reach for her. She drifted in and out of clubs, became a model with a platinum-blonde hair-do, made money enough to afford a comfortable Kensington flat, and when she went to bed alone it was with the feeling that she was doing all right for little Ruthie.

Then she put her arms round a tall handsome young man with dark curly hair and a dazzling smile and stepped on to the dance floor with him. When she stepped off she was still with him, and bells were ringing in the ears under the platinum hair.

This was it. This was the real thing. It had come to her a little later in life than to Kitty Byron, and she had taken time out to have a few flings around the romantic mulberry-bush, but she knew love when it made her heart thump, just as Kitty Byron had. For Ruth Ellis what she felt for David Blakely, who liked fast women and loved faster cars, was love. She told him, and he believed her, or said he did.

She was three years older than this man who could push up a fine turn of speed at Le Mans and Goodwood, and had driven one winter in the Monte Carlo rally. He came of an active family. He had brothers who were pilots. He also had a background enriched with hard cash. His stepfather had made a fortune with his own textile business.

There was, however, a worm in the apple, although Ruth Ellis was not prepared to let the fact stop her from nibbling another woman's fruit. Blakely was engaged to a very likeable girl whose family had social standing and the wealth to prove it.

Like a good many men of strong appetites, Blakely liked to have his cake and to be able to consume it at the same time. With Ruth Ellis this culinary impossibility seemed in a high degree possible, which was gratifying.

So, eschewing apples and cake and other metaphors more pertaining to a picnic, Blakely and Ruth Ellis let passion have its head and make its own speed. It was quite breathtaking. They rushed around together in a whirl of pleasure and romantic pantomime that made the days speed past like trees beyond the window of an express train.

Although Blakely's home was in Buckinghamshire, he spent most of his time with her during those first months when they appeared to have so much for each other. Neither apparently realized, for all their vaunted sophistication, that a candle burning at both ends gutters twice as fast. To the woman Blakely was her life. To the man Ruth Ellis was a part of his life, never more than that. There was always, waiting for him, that other world of friends and motor-racing. He could return to it by simply picking up a phone and asking how's tricks.

In time it was this other world that tore at him to return. The world of Ruth Ellis, of passion quickly sated, of long bouts of waiting between meetings, of over-bright sparkle and accented glamour, its appeal thinned. There was always, for David Blakely, the reality of the auto circuit, and the smell of axle grease and lubricating oil at times had more appeal for his senses than French perfume.

If Ruth Ellis understood the truth of this she did not accept it. She made the mistake of trying to combat it, to put herself before the older and deeper loves.

Their quarrels graduated from a few words to high old rows. Blakely hated tears. He found, as others had before him, that they cooled his ardour fast. It would have been different if he had been genuinely in love with the woman, if she had meant to him a companion for the remainder of his life. She didn't. She was a good-time companion, and he liked her one hell of a lot, and told her so, but he never got around to telling her she was the only woman in the world.

He knew she wasn't.

So, with Easter 1955 in sight, Ruth Ellis found herself not only having a miscarriage but drifting towards that loneliness of heart and home that would come with a permanent break. She knew Blakely was easing himself out of her life, although he professed to be as keenly attached to her as ever. She decided she couldn't continue in this way. She had lived at speed with Blakely, and she would sooner crash than slam on the brake.

So she forced him to promise to see her over the Easter, and he said he would, although she knew he was racing at Goodwood on the Monday of the holiday and would be caught up in arrangements with his racing friends. He was entered as driver of an Emperor H.R.G. But the more she thought about it, the more she told herself she couldn't wait until after the race. She had to know where she stood with Blakely before the race, before the Monday.

She sat out that first week of April after her miscarriage, and had a bad time. When she got up on the Good Friday, April 8th, her nerve was badly shot. To steady it she opened a fresh bottle of Pernod. Before she stepped out later she had finished it.

She picked up the phone in her Egerton Gardens flat and dialled a number she hated. She went on dialling it at intervals, always to be informed that Blakely was not there. The masculine voice that spoke to her became more annoyed each time it answered her question. Then came the discovery that someone in the other apartment had taken the receiver out of its cradle. It was as though Blakely was utterly lost to her.

She sat through some of the loneliest hours of her life then, trying to understand herself, hoping there would be a ring and Blakely would speak to her as he had promised.

She cried and came through tears to dry-eyed heart-ache, and then she went to the drawer where she kept the gun. It was one of a large number of similar small arms sent to Britain from the United States as lend-lease during the recent war. The gun had been left with her as pledge for a debt by a man who had entered her life for a brief spell and left it like a phantom. She had never removed the bullets. There had been a number on the gun, but she could not read it because it had been overstamped, which suggested that someone for his own doubtless good enough reason had wanted the gun to be officially lost.

Well, it had been as good as lost in Ruth Ellis's drawer. But now it was lost no longer. It was about to feature in a murder trial at the Old Bailey, and a Scotland Yard forensic scientist was to put the weapon under his microscope and discover that the over-stamped number was, in fact, 9915.

Not that the woman in Egerton Gardens grasping the gun in her right hand that Good Friday evening ever became interested in the weapon's antecedents. When she dropped it back in the drawer she knew she was soon to walk into a cul-de-sac from which she might not be able to turn round and walk back. But then she didn't wish to be able to walk back if she ever took that gun for company.

She wanted to end this kind of living that had grown unbearable, and one sure way of doing that was to kill David Blakely.

When she thought of the act she went cold. But she was not repelled by the thought, nor was she afraid of the deed.

It would mean destroying herself, but she had been telling herself that without David Blakely she didn't want to go on living. She believed that ardently as Good Friday waned. There is no reason to suppose she ever changed her mind.

She tortured herself by another attempt to reach Blakely on the phone, only to hear the unobtainable signal mocking her with a rhythm that throbbed like a drum-beat through her auditory canal.

She slammed down the receiver, knowing that somehow a decision had been demanded of her. She picked up her handbag and left her flat in Egerton Gardens. She hastened to another flat. She knew the address very well. It was in Tanza Road, Hampstead, and it had a telephone with a receiver out of its cradle. She knew, just as surely as though she had second sight or the ability to see through brick as through glass, that David Blakely was there, forgetting her.

She went to the door of the flat, pounded on it. No one came to answer. She rang the bell, with the same result. She stood back and shouted. She was angry and frustrated and she sounded like a fishwife.

Someone summoned the police.

She was advised to desist and to leave. She was making a nuisance of herself.

Had her brain been functioning normally the irony must have struck her. She had every intention of making a considerable nuisance of herself—to one man. In fact, if he continued to avoid her she would make herself the ultimate nuisance.

Although she left the flat in Tanza Road, it was not for long. She didn't need another shot of Pernod now. She had to see Blakely if it was possible before she found herself with only a reason for killing him because there was nothing else she could do.

Her mind was revolving like a Catherine wheel.

She went back to the flat, pounded on the door and called. The door did not open. Beyond it the voices and laughter made a drone of sound that was sheer mockery. Defeated, she turned and stumbled out into the street, where Blakely's Vanguard was parked at the kerb. There had been times in that car when she had been deliriously happy. She went up to it and slung her handbag. The smashed triplex of the windows tinkled to the ground.

Then she went home.

Saturday was an evil day. Blakely did not ring, and she could not reach him.

Sunday she consumed more Pernod steadily. Towards evening she went to the drawer containing the gun, took it out, and put the weapon in her handbag. She felt cold but determined. She was not prepared to live through any more dreadful days like these, consumed by a jealousy with teeth that ripped her mind to red shreds. Blakely had promised to get in touch with her and his promise meant nothing to him. True, she had kicked up the fuss on Good Friday, but a man who loved a woman was understanding. Blakely should know why she had been compelled to go to Tanza Road. He should understand what had driven her.

Well, there was still time to bring him understanding. That was more important than drinking with his pals or racing at Goodwood on Easter Monday.

She started back to Tanza Road.

She stood outside the house and looked up. It was a warm night and the window of the Findlaters' flat was open. From inside came sounds of a party. She remained in the street, waiting. She was there when Blakely and some of his friends came out of the flat, and Blakely called over his shoulder, 'We'll collect some fresh bottles and be right back.'

She knew where the bottles would be collected, at the Magdala public house in South Hill Park, Hampstead. She walked there at her own pace, looked through the window of a bar, and saw Blakely with his head thrown back laughing. Blakely and a friend came out into the street. Almost at once there was the sound of shooting. Alan Thompson, a police constable, was off duty that Sunday night and sitting in the pub having a glass of beer. As soon as he heard the shots he ran out. He saw a man lying on the pavement close to a parked car. A woman with silvery blonde hair was bending over him. She held a gun she had emptied of bullets. She let Thompson take it from her and said in a tight little whisper, 'Phone the police.'

She was tried before Mr. Justice Havers at the Old Bailey. The turning point of that trial came when Mr. Christmas Humphreys, who led for the prosecution, asked Dr. Duncan Whittaker, a well-known psychiatrist, 'In your view, there was such emotional tension over that week-end without relief that she was impelled to resort to violent action to relieve that suppressed emotion?'

'Yes,' said the psychiatrist.

'In your view was she, in the meaning of English law, sane or insane at the time?'

'Sane.'

There was no reprieve for Ruth Ellis as for Kitty Byron. No one offered to take her place on the gallows, although petitions were sent to Parliament. She was hanged on Wednesday, July 13th.

11 * The Love Vampire

Jeanne Amenaide Brécourt was one of the most deadly women who ever lived, yet she did not commit murder. She was far too cunning. She induced her victims to commit suicide. Yet she was as guilty as though she had plunged a knife into their hearts.

At least, so thought the famous Gustave Macé, who came to be head of the Sûreté.

Moreover, Jeanne Brécourt enjoyed being guilty. She not only considered each death she caused a sufficient reason for feeling pleased with herself, but she accepted it as a tribute to her arts of love, for her victims killed themselves in the despair she inserted in their lives, like a spreading cancer, after she had been their mistress.

She was born in 1837, that year when the young Victoria mounted the throne of England and began ruling throughout an age that was to be known by her name. Her family lived in Paris, and were of sound artisan stock. Her father was a printer, and her mother had her own trade of selling vegetables in Les Halles, still today the vaunted stomach of the French capital, the sprawling food-and-produce market. If the mother with a stall to tend did not have the time necessary to devote to the upbringing of her small daughter she soon learned that it would be better to make time. For even as a very small child Jeanne Brécourt was wayward to the point of being destructive when she couldn't have her own way.

It is related that she was very young when she was given a frock she did not like because its colour did not appeal to her young Parisienne's eye. She stamped her feet and yelled to her mother that she would not wear it. Her mother told her she would.

What might have been considered a stalemate produced by a childish tantrum was solved in a grimly adult way that was completely final. The child found a pair of scissors and cut the offending frock to scraps. At a very early age she learned that a violent eruption did one thing for her. It allowed her to keep her word. The frock was cut to pieces before it had been worn.

Not unnaturally the child who could perform so devastatingly was no shy little mademoiselle. She was bright and perky, and took the eye of a woman of means with no children of her own. This woman approached the Brécourt parents and made them an offer. If they would relinquish Jeanne to her she would adopt the girl, ensure that she received a good education, and bring her up as though she were her daughter.

To Jeanne's parents the proposal had a great deal to commend it. They could free themselves of Jeanne's displays of temper while feeling they had agreed to an arrangement that would materially benefit the girl herself.

So Jeanne was adopted by a baroness whose eye had been captivated by the perky youngster with her fresh looks. Precisely what kind of education the girl acquired is not known, but it must be supposed that her benefactress's interest waned as Jeanne lost such winsomeness as she had as a child and grew to be an insolent teenager. We know that by the time she was seventeen Jeanne was working in a silk factory, which is hardly the employment one would expect for a girl brought up by a baroness as her own daughter. There is the possibility, of course, that a Peke or a Chow or even a poodle had superseded a mere child in appeal for the titled woman of leisure. However that may be, Jeanne had received a close-up of how the other half lives, and she liked the view and remembered it when in the silk factory. Her ambition was to quit work and never return to what she considered drudgery.

Other young females have had the same ambition. Few attained it in the manner pursued by Jeanne Brécourt.

The first move was conventional enough. She married at eighteen a man said to be old enough to be her father. His name was Graz and he was a grocer. He very soon discovered that the most spicy object in his *epicerie* was the wife who began to make his life miserable with her cantankerous ways, her readiness to create a scene and to quarrel, and her constant demands for money. Jeanne found that she could do better than stand up to her husband's threats, she could come to blows and expect to win in a toe-to-toe contest. After that the grocer's life became unendurable. He sold out and took flight.

Not that Jeanne sat moping because she found herself deserted. She took off herself, and for a while appeared in a number of the more risqué theatrical productions. She also tried to win acceptance as a journalist writing about the seamy side of life. But in this she was about seventy years before her time.

She left Paris for the provinces, and when she came back she had shed her last threadbare illusions. She settled down to let her looks provide her with a livelihood. It was an age of flourishing courtesans, when fine feathers were reputed to make fine birds, and the nicest of women had moments when they envied some of the pleasure enjoyed by their more unscrupulous and undoubtedly more energetic sisters.

Jeanne Brécourt, as she reverted to calling herself, possibly because she did not wish to be reminded of the vanished grocer, began a veritable career of making men pay for what she believed to be the wrongs she had already suffered. She certainly had some inflated values and these might have applied equally to those fancied wrongs, for one cannot suppose the galloping grocer was in a very strong position for wronging anyone except himself when he married a forceful and fanciful young woman who loved him about as much as she did too much salt in her potage.

But it is possible to accept what Jeanne Brécourt had become because the young woman who had tried her hand at journalism did not lose the urge to write in later years, and what she put down for her own delectation and delight is most revealing. She had one perennial subject—men.

On the subject in general she wrote:

> 'To me the world is a vast chessboard, on which men are the pawns I move as I please, and when I weary of them I break them or fling them aside. The more I break, the more pleased

and happy I am. They have served their purpose and—puf!—I look out for the next.'

She could even be repetitive on the subject, for she also wrote:

'Everything in this world is lies and dust. So much the worse for the men who get in my path. As soon as they fail me or bore me or are played out in regard to what they can spend on me, I have no further use for them.'

Certainly revealing comments to make about oneself, but then Jeanne Brécourt was making a career of bringing acute suffering to dupes who had the folly to consider themselves in love with her. It was the age when Cora Pearl was queen of Paris, and duelling with whips any woman who contested the title. Jeanne Brécourt, the one-time protegée of a baroness, became a kind of poor man's Cora Pearl, with her own savage undertones. These were deadly.

Cora Pearl wanted only money and position. She moved in a high-toned and high-titled world as a professional *femme entretenue*, to be kept in exclusivity by one protector—at a time, that is. Jeanne Brécourt wanted more than money, and she did not care very much about position so long as she had the comfort money guaranteed its possessor. She wanted to degrade the men who bought her favours or sold themselves to her, as she preferred to invert the meaning of the relationship. She was something more than a prostitute, not quite a courtesan, for whereas the former is in the market to be purchased, the latter is almost fastidious in the selection of her patrons.

Jeanne Brécourt could be bought for the right price if she could choose her own terms.

Her life was a very full one. It was also a very profitable one. Each romantic excursion ended with her credit in a more healthy condition, and with another hapless male in the depths of despair and contemplating suicide as the one real solution to his misery.

For she became an accomplished blackmailer. At least one man killed himself because she turned the blackmail screw too tightly. Another, afraid that his family would learn of his wild indulgences with this professional purveyor of passion, went out of his mind and had to be placed in an asylum. She was a past-mistress in her erotic cult, and her supply of victims rarely gave out or even threatened to, for there were plenty of young fools in the Paris of her day to feel that a whirl with Jeanne Brécourt was something to brag about. Parents went to the police. They could do nothing. Her victims refused to talk because she had filled them with shame.

Feeling that she could do better with a title, she gave herself one. She took a more fancy apartment and became the Baroness de la Cour, probably a title that was a lasting souvenir of the real baroness whose daughter she didn't quite become. She went to Vittel, but not to enjoy the waters. There was nothing wrong with her health, only with the health of the dupes and dullards who allowed themselves to become infatuated with her smooth, polished looks and strong sensual appeal.

She was at the spa when she received news of the death of the one-time grocer who had panicked. The late Monsieur Graz had little to leave his widow except her freedom. She very quickly decided to hock it.

She returned to Paris and looked around. That meant continuing her career of love vampire, as she was termed later. She brought her diary up to date. There was a fresh unnamed victim who spent his last franc on her and left her to take his own life, all she had left him. When she heard of his death she wrote: 'Thank heaven. That's one man less!' It was as though she had resolved to decimate the male population of the city. Another of her victims was not quite so determined. He attempted to find consolation in strong waters, but died in poverty of *delirium tremens*. She managed to keep track of these devastated ruins of men and invariably gloated over her achievement and recorded her victim's degradation. When yet another of her victims died in hospital she appended a note to his brief history in her life describing him as 'a fool who has only got his deserts'.

There was also Alphonse. His other name is not known, but at a later date countless readers of her diary knew his sad, trumpery saga.

Some time after Alphonse was snared by this Diana of the human chase and was hopelessly entangled she wrote:

'Today Alphonse came to see me and behaved in the most extraordinary manner. He grovelled at my feet, sobbed as if his heart was breaking—as I dare say it was—and implored me not to desert him, but to love him, however little. I could have screamed with laughter, he looked so comical. I wondered how I could ever have had anything to do with such a booby.

But of course he had money—and money I must have at any cost. And so I have had it—all he had got. I had no more use for him. I told him so, and he swore that he would commit suicide.

I told him that was his concern, not mine—but he must go elsewhere to do it. Without a word he rushed out of the room, and I laughed.

How I laughed!'

A few days later she didn't bother to laugh. Alphonse had been relegated to the past tense, even by himself.

She penned this brief notice that was her memorial to a lost lover with empty pockets:

'Have just heard that Alphonse's body has been taken out of the Seine. So he really meant it after all! I didn't think Alphonse had the will to do it—the poor fool.'

That diary, when eventually it came to be read, was found to contain the record of no less than twenty-one lovers whose lives she had wrecked and whose money she had filched or squandered.

Neither age nor youth deterred her or withheld her from her curiously compulsive purpose of wrecking men's lives because they were men.

Jean-Baptiste Carlier was only nineteen. At the time of his tragic entanglement with her she was old enough to be his mother. When she told him she 'had no more use for him' he shot himself and left his widowed mother broken-hearted. Louis Carnot, a retired civil servant, was seventy-four. She made him feel spring had blossomed again in his life, and he spent all his savings on her before she laughingly told him he was an old goat. It is recorded that he died of starvation somewhere in the then very unfashionable village of Montmartre.

Perhaps in the light of her relentless persistence in pursuing victims it is not surprising that her mind, for a while, became affected by her obsession in destroying the other sex. She evinced signs of instability that resulted in her own sojourn for a while in an asylum. According to her own words, written later, she was 'a prey to terrifying and torturing delusions'. But away from men the tension that had distorted her mind relaxed and she returned to a state that for her was normal. She left the asylum, and again in her own apartment found that her dissipations and excesses had left their mark on her.

The beauty that had made her chosen way of life easy was blurred. The brightness had gone from her eyes, which were hard and narrow as her mouth was thin and unable to conceal its expression of cruelty.

She realized she had set out to find a husband with a fortune, but had forgotten her secondary quest in her eagerness to obtain ready tribute from temporary victims who provided her sadistic nature with the kind of obsessive sport that had almost destroyed her mind. She tried to take herself in hand. She became even more determinedly the bogus Baroness de la Cour, and, realizing that with fading looks and filling figure, her allure would be less obvious, and that she would therefore be less able to make her blackmail racket pay the dividends it had hitherto, she gave herself to looking for a dupe who might be worth leading to the altar.

Her gaze fastened on Georges de Saint-Pierre. He was twenty, she nearly twice that age. He was also the son of a family of good standing, and might be said to enjoy what in those days was referred to as expectations.

With great concentration and with a most deceptive tenderness she set herself to snare the young Georges, and she succeeded, but not as far as the altar. She found that she could not bring herself to marry again. It was as though she, who had dominated so many men, including her mouse of a wedded mate, feared that by marrying for a second time she would be gambling with her luck.

This was a curious and disturbing reversal of her normal most positive role, and it not only puzzled her but left her unsure of herself. For this reason she would not release her emotional hold on Georges de Saint-Pierre. In fact, she remained his mistress for three years, taking every care to keep him from discovering the truth about her. So far as Georges knew, she was a lovely widow who had battled against a stormy and unrelenting Fate to keep herself unsullied.

Early in their association he had written her: 'Your form is ever before my eyes. I wish I could enshrine your pure heart in gold and crystal.'

They were days of extravagant and flowery speeches, but young Georges de Saint-Pierre was in a class by himself when it came to writing romantic drivel.

Three years later he could contrive to write this, and not with his tongue in his much-kissed cheek:

> 'It is enough for me that you love me, because I don't weary you; and I—I love you with all my heart. I cannot bear to leave you. I don't know what would become of me if I did not feel that your love watched over me.'

In not a great while he was to find out what could become of him when what he called her love for him was watching over him—too closely. Jeanne Brécourt watched Georges because she knew that his family now realized he had a mistress and disapproved. They wanted him to marry a young woman of his own class, and he would not mention Jeanne to them, fearful of their reaction. But in their own way his family began to exert pressure on him by making demands on his loyalty and time. He wrote Jeanne a letter assuring her he would never change towards her whatever his family did or said. He even added with a flourish: 'I cannot bear the thought of leaving you, and I don't intend to. We will live together and defy them to do their worst.'

After three years, for this stage to be reached was a shattering revelation to the woman approaching forty. Perhaps, after all, she should force herself to go through the uncertainty of another marriage. Perhaps she was a fool to think it could change her luck. But she knew what she really feared. The possibility of a young husband deserting her. The timid grocer had been no loss when she was young. But the passing years had changed too much for her to take desertion in her stride a second time. It would be too wounding to her pride—as well as her purse.

Then chance gave her a terrible and terrifying idea.

She was visited by an actress friend who had married a blind man, and Jeanne noted with excited interest the husband's utter dependence on his wife. She had to be his eyes. His awareness of the world beyond his reach was limited to what she told him.

Jeanne Brécourt considered what it would mean for Georges de Saint-Pierre to be dependent on her in the same way.

The practical-minded woman of the theatre demonstrated just how practical her outlook was when she told Jeanne Brécourt: 'I don't mind being pitied for marrying a blind husband, for there are advantages. I don't have to worry if he will leave me—he can't. He thinks he's lucky, for I've told him no one else would marry him. As for me, I can come and go as I choose. Why not? Who can do anything about it?'

The terrible and terrifying idea was a mental picture of Saint-Pierre purposely blinded in order to ensure his dependence on her. She quickly saw that to achieve this she would need help, and from an unscrupulous accomplice, if one could be found. She went over her list of acquaintances and reached the name of Nathalis Gaudry, whom she had known when working in the silk factory. She made inquiries, learned that he had completed his military service and then gone adventuring from one country to another, but was back in Paris, employed in an oil refinery. Cautiously she sought him out, but immediately they met there was no need for her caution.

Gaudry greeted her like an old friend and promptly felt the tug of that resilient allure that other men had known and Georges de Saint-Pierre was currently experiencing after being held in thrall by it for three years. Gaudry was older, his eyes were sharp, his wits nimble. He knew the allure was there and that the woman who possessed it well understood its value in francs. He understood also that she hadn't taken the trouble to find him after a long lapse of years because she was interested to know if he still had all his teeth.

It wasn't long before Gaudry sucked his breath sharply in well-nigh stupefied surprise. Jeanne Brécourt wanted him to act the jealous lover in earnest. She even had her plot all prepared. He was to throw the contents of a bottle of vitriol in the face of a young man named Saint-Pierre. To his own amazement Gaudry found himself agreeing to be her accomplice in an act that made him shudder, and he couldn't pretend he did not know why.

Jeanne Brécourt was lavish with her promises of the delights in store for the man who came to her aid, as she described what she wanted done.

The details were carefully explained to the receptive Gaudry. She had already procured some oil of vitriol on the pretext of requiring it to clean some metalware. One evening Gaudry was to conceal himself behind a small pavilion next to the house where she had her apartment, and wait till she returned home from the theatre with Saint-Pierre. The signal would be Saint-Pierre's stepping ahead of her to open a gate. She would keep back, and Gaudry could then make his surprise attack with the vitriol.

Had Gaudry not been a ruffian by nature he could not have contemplated performing the despicable role she had cast him for, but she overcame such timid scruples as he possessed by appealing blatantly to his strong sensuality.

At the time she planned with Gaudry the young man who was to be the victim of their plot was away at his family's country home. When he returned to Paris she told herself she detected a change in him, and wondered how strong had been the parental arguments to induce him to leave his unknown mistress.

Pretending to be anxious to cheer him up, she arranged that they should go to the opera. She sent word to Gaudry, who came and received the bottle of vitriol and his final instructions. On the day she and Georges de Saint-Pierre were to go to the opera in the evening she expressed a longing for some fresh air. They went to the Bois and joined the fashionable strollers. That afternoon must have passed on tired feet for the impatient love-vampire.

The time spent at the opera must have dragged even more slowly. It certainly did for Gaudry. But the man with a bottle of vitriol and implicit instructions what to do with it was waiting by the pavilion when Saint-Pierre rattled the catch of the gate. As the young man turned to take the first steps up the path beyond, a speeding shadow descended upon him. He turned in surprise to receive the contents of Gaudry's raised bottle full in the face.

With a loud cry of pain Saint-Pierre ran gropingly towards the house at the end of the path, calling: 'I am blind. Oh, my God, I am blind!'

He did not see his assailant's face, and by the time he was

stumbling up to the door Gaudry had gone through the gate with the rattling catch and had disappeared.

Jeanne Brécourt put on one of her best performances as an actress. She became intensely feminine, weeping hysterically and pretending to be helpless as she shrieked for assistance. Passers-by and police arrived to find her apparently in a state of collapse at the side of the moaning huddle that was Georges de Saint-Pierre.

When the police began asking questions she had herself well under control. Still behaving as though the attack was a complete mystery, she appeared bemused and distrait.

'It must have been some awful mistake,' she insisted to the police. 'Some crazy person must have mistaken Monsieur Saint-Pierre for another man.'

Certainly the young man himself accepted this explanation. He was confined to a sick-bed for weeks, and Jeanne Brécourt made a show of nursing him and being very gentle and full of compassion, so that he called her his guardian angel. The inroads made on his resolve to stay with her by his family were more than discounted by the designing woman, who saw that, given a little more time, she might well expect Sainte-Pierre to marry her, provided she could arrange for the suggestion to appear to come from the blinded man.

Her one problem, it seemed, was her accomplice.

Nathalis Gaudry was the kind of man who expected payment to be made promptly, and she was in his debt very considerably. Unless she was able to appease his demands he was capable of endangering the final success of her scheme to provide adequate insurance for her advancing years.

So she made arrangements for clandestine meetings with her accomplice, and at her most persuasive she managed to gain time and calm his impatience to receive fulfilment of her exciting promises.

However, one thing she did not know. Her meetings with Gaudry were reported by a detective sent to watch her movements by Gustave Macé, who was the local *commissaire*, and one who had already displayed that brilliant detective flair which marked him as an exception among manhunters by solving the famous Voirbo case and the mystery of the limbs found in a Paris well.

Macé had read the report of the police about an acid attack.

Something about the sequence of events seemed wrong to his searching mind. He couldn't understand why Saint-Pierre should be going ahead through the gate and up the path when he was accompanied by a female. The most natural thing would have been for him to have opened the gate and stood back to allow her to pass in front of him, and when Macé found the most natural thing was almost determinedly avoided he became suspicious. Not without reason, as he usually discovered in a long life of combating crime and criminals.

In the present case of the acid-throwing, for example, the couple could have had a quarrel, and an angry woman was capable of anything, depending on her anger and the woman. From what he was able to learn of rumours about Jeanne Brécourt she was one to be watched.

So the meetings with Gaudry were reported. Gaudry's background was checked. The old association with Jeanne Brécourt seemed highly significant when the present furtive meetings were considered. Saint-Pierre's family were visited. There Macé found only enmity towards the young man's hidden mistress. The *commissaire* consulted a *juge d'instruction*, and in his company called at Jeanne Brécourt's apartment.

She put on a thoroughly indignant act, demanding the names of the persons responsible for such a visit.

Macé was impressed, but not for the reason the aroused woman supposed. He decided he could do little at the moment save watch and wait. When Jeanne left to join Saint-Pierre at Corbevoie, not a great distance from Paris, a detective was told to follow. Saint-Pierre was completely blind in one eye and the sight of the other was greatly impaired. He was only a pathetic wraith of the young man of a few weeks before the acid attack. Macé received word that Jeanne Brécourt had again gone into her ministering angel act.

He applied for a warrant for her arrest. With this as authority he searched her apartment in her absence, and discovered one of the most nauseating collections of correspondence ever seen by the cynical eye of an experienced police officer.

There were letters describing wild erotic adventures, letters cursing an evil woman who had destroyed their writers, letters containing the tenderest endearments—in all a veritable manuscript library to Jeanne Brécourt's years of exploiting and duping her lovers. There was even a black-edged mourning card on which the sender had scrawled: 'Jeanne, in the flush of my youth, I die because of you—but I forgive you.' And there was one parcel of scorched letters. These were from Saint-Pierre. They had every appearance to Macé of having been thrown on a fire at someone's behest, and then surreptitiously recovered. Their contents would have lain the writer open to moral blackmail for the rest of his life.

Jeanne Brécourt was arrested by detectives, and Macé went personally to explain to the numbed and wholly incredible Saint-Pierre why he had acted as he had. Only after the *commissaire* had torn the last figurative scales from the blinded eyes which could not see the visitor clearly did Saint-Pierre accept the horrible truth. He had been worshipping a woman of incredible evil. He told Macé how he had begged her to burn his letters because he felt ashamed, when with his family, of having written such obscene passages as they contained.

Jeanne Brécourt was kept in the prison of Saint-Lazare, where she was sufficiently incautious to write a warning note to Gaudry. She tried to have it smuggled out, but it fell into the hands of the prison authorities, and Gaudry was promptly arrested. Aware of his precarious position, he made a detailed confession, claiming he had done what he had because he was obsessively infatuated with the woman whose scheme he had carried out. Receiving word of this betrayal, as she considered it, Jeanne Brécourt twice tried to commit suicide in her dismal cell by swallowing powdered glass and verdigris. Her unsuccessful efforts revealed that she was less adept at bringing about her own suicide than the suicides of others.

On May 12th, 1877, she was confronted by Gaudry, who swore, 'She told me Saint-Pierre had treated her very badly, and I felt justified in aiding her vengeance.' She called him a liar, which was a mistake. Hard-faced and hard-tongued, Jeanne Brécourt had no vestige of feminine charm. Gaudry stuck to his confession and his motive for helping her.

The trial of the sordid pair opened on June 23rd, and lasted for three days, during which time Jeanne Brécourt was defended in a most spirited manner by Maître Lauchad, one of the most eminent advocates of his time. But he could not minimize her complicity. On the other hand Maître Demange, who appeared for Gaudry, and had the reputation of being able to sway susceptible juries with his eloquence, successfully presented his client as a simple-hearted man who had been tricked by a designing and sensuous woman.

The prisoners were found guilty, Jeanne Brécourt being sentenced to fifteen years' penal servitude and Gaudry, now recognized as the tool she had handled, to the comparatively light term of five. Between them they had demonstrated that a bottle of vitriol can be a devastating weapon. Its uses are still being recalled occasionally nearly a century later.

12 * The Mail Order Circe

It was on the morning of Tuesday, April 28th, 1908, that an Indiana farmhand named Joe Maxson woke early and smelled smoke. It wasn't yet light as he sat up in bed rinsing his face in his hands and collecting his sleep-drugged senses. His first thought was the very human one of 'Hot cakes for breakfast—good', and then he saw it was still night outside his window.

He slept in a room that was over the farmhouse kitchen. When he reached the window and peered out he was startled to see flames licking up from below. He rushed to a door connecting the frame building housing the kitchen and his own sleeping quarters with the main structure of the brick-built farmhouse. But he couldn't open it. The connecting door was locked.

He began yelling, 'Fire, fire!' hoping to stir the sleeping family. The only reply was the now audible crackle of the flames below. Joe decided there was no sense in staying to be fried. He rushed back to his room, pulled on his boots, snatched his clothes from their pegs and hastily packed his valise with the few possessions he owned. Almost sobbing for fear he wouldn't make it, Joe hurled himself down the stairs, dodging the red tongues of the crackling flames and rushed into what remained of a spring night.

As he ran around the house he saw three figures hurrying to join him. They were young Bill Clifford, his father Mike, from the nearest farm, and William Humphrey, Mike Clifford's brother-in-law. They threw some bricks at the window of the family's bedroom when Maxson pointed it out. Glass tinkled, but no heads appeared.

The flames crept from the furiously blazing kitchen section to the brick farmhouse, caught at timbers, stole through broken windows, began to eat at wooden stairs and furniture. By daylight the house was past saving. But so far there had been no sign of the woman who owned the farm. A large knot of people from other farms arrived. They could do little to combat the flames. By midday the farmhouse was gutted, and everyone standing and staring at the smoking ruins had one question to which there was seemingly no answer.

Where was Belle Gunness?

By mid-afternoon Deputies Leroy Marr and William Anstiss from La Porte had taken over. They gave the word to start digging in the blackened ruins. By half past four the searchers had found nothing, and most of the crowd of sightseers had drifted away. Shortly afterwards, with only two spectators present, a digger's shovel turned over a fire-blackened head. It was a small head, a child's. Belle Gunness, the owner of the farm, was the twice-bereaved mother of three children.

Myrtle was eleven, Lucy nine, and Philip five.

The diggers uncovered the remainder of the burned child's body. It was that of one of Mrs. Gunness's little girls. The other girl's body was found close by, and not far from the charred remains of the sisters the diggers next uncovered the burned-black body of a woman, with the remains of a small boy against her.

The four corpses were arranged almost neatly, but with one surprising and startling omission.

The burned corpse of the woman had no head.

The men who dug among the ruins of the Gunness farm felt they had to find the head. After all, even a fire-blackened skull cannot disappear, and when the remains of the fire's victims were buried it would be seemly to include the woman's head with her body.

So they sifted among still-smouldering beams and turned over mounds of blackened brickwork that had collapsed. They did not find the head belonging to the woman's body, but their spades drove through soft earth under ground that had been scorched by the fire, and they came upon the body of a man. The fire had not touched his remains. He had been buried some time before the fire gutted the farmhouse. The body wore no clothing, and the trench in which it had been found was very obviously a grave.

When Asle Helgelien saw the face of the man whose grave had been uncovered he cried, 'That's my brother.'

Whatever had caused Andrew Helgelien's death, his burial was impressive. His legs and arms had been separated from his torso and wrapped in sacking. His head had been separately packaged also, and a dealer recognized the covering as one of his grain sacks.

The local sheriff ordered the diggers to keep on with their work. They cleared a rubbish dump and about four feet below came upon piles of human bones, which were taken to the shed where the farm buggy had been kept. There were the bones of four persons in the pile left in the shed. Next to the shed was an apple-tree in blossom. It provided a contrast in incongruity.

One of the bodies was found to be Jennie Olsen's, a blonde girl of sixteen whom Belle Gunness had adopted, and who, it was checked, had not been seen in the La Porte district since September, 1906, more than eighteen months before. Of the other three bodies one was that of a man with a fountain of red whiskers adhering to his fleshless head, one was of a smaller man, and the remaining body was a woman's.

All had been cut up neatly and the pieces packaged. It was not only gruesome, it was wholesale, and it was unquestionably murder.

The district became invaded by a host of newspaper reporters when the discovery at the gutted Gunness farm was broadcast. The idea of a female multiple murderess was blood-chilling, and sufficiently unique to make national headline news. The headlines eventually reached not only across the width of the United States but round the entire world. The name of Belle Gunness became universally notorious. The fair-haired Scandinavian woman who married men for their money and then butchered them and disposed of the carcasses still stands unique in the annals of mass murder.

'The Mail Order Circe' one garish headline proclaimed her when her story was written up after police investigations had filled in parts not even suspected. It provides the key to the riddle of a woman who was never brought to justice.

For on that night of the fire, which brought her bloody trade to the public's appalled gaze, she vanished and was never found.

It was her sister, living in Chicago, some sixty miles from La Porte, who gave the police the background story on Bella Poulsdatter. She was a Norwegian, born in 1859 beside Lake Selbe, close to Trondhjem. Her father had been a stonemason, and after his son joined him in that craft the elder sister emigrated to the United States. When she had become Mrs. John Larson she wrote her sister Bella to come and join her. Her husband sent the younger sister's passage money. So in 1883 Bella Poulsdatter arrived in the States and altered her name to Belle Poulson, but after a year she changed it again, this time to Mrs. Sorenson.

She passionately wanted children, but none were born to her and her blond giant of a husband, and she tried to persuade the Larsons to let her adopt a niece. However, the Larsons rejected the idea and the niece herself revealed plainly that she did not care for her buxom Aunt Belle. The upshot was strained relations between the Norwegian sisters, and they kept carefully out of each other's way.

Mads Sorenson was a guard in a Chicago department store. He made no fuss when Belle adopted some other children, but she seemed to be a woman dogged with misfortune. No less than three times her home was destroyed by fire and she lost practically all her belongings. The childless marriage lasted for seventeen years, when Mads Sorenson died quite suddenly and unexpectedly. He was well insured, however, and his widow drew a sum of money that for a while left her comfortably off.

That was in 1900.

With her three foster daughters, Jennie, Myrtle, and Lucy, she went to La Porte, where she had heard of a farm for sale. It was about a mile north of the Indiana town, on the McClung road. A woman named Mattie Altic had run the square red-brick farmhouse as a bordello, and at one time its reputation was quite salty. Belle Sorenson, a widow with three girls and her own buxom good looks, moved in after completing the purchase, and the neighbours wondered what she was going to do there on her own. They didn't have to wonder very long. She took a trip one day, and when she returned was accompanied by a tall light-haired man named Peter Gunness. He had blue eyes and straw-coloured face whiskers and he carried a baby in his arms. The baby was his by his first marriage.

His second had been to Belle Sorenson.

So the newly-weds with four children settled down in the solid brick farmhouse and gave it their name. It became known as the Gunness farm. But curiously, as the records turned up, Belle's erstwhile misfortune continued to dog her well-planted steps.

Within a year she was again a widow. Peter Gunness's baby died first, then its father. The latter had an accident in the middle of the night. For some quite unexplained reason he chose this most unusual hour to examine a kettle of brine that was used for pickling pork. While he was satisfying himself about the brine the big-bladed cutter from a sausage-meat grinder fell on his head, and Belle Gunness had to unpack her widow's weeds.

The neighbours from farms close by came and offered the buxom blonde Norse woman their condolences. Some of them were of Scandinavian stock like herself and her dead husbands. Their sympathy was warm, and they offered material help in getting the farm running for a widow woman with children to bring up.

But Belle Gunness thanked them and went about running things herself, without taking any well-meant advice. The neighbours shook their heads. They could see that she was pregnant. When the child was not far from arrival into the curious world of the red-brick house where gay old times had been lived by Mattie Altic's girls and their customers some of the neighbours' wives decided to do their Christian duty by taking their unwanted advice back to the obstinate daughter of Vikings. They arrived to find she had delivered herself of a man child she was going to have christened Philip, and the next day was scrubbing the family wash at a large tub.

'You should be resting in bed,' they told her.

She gave them her hard bright blue stare.

'Why?' she said, in genuine surprise. 'Women don't go to bed like that in the Old Country.'

She made a real job of cleaning up the run-down house, and gradually, hiring labour when she could afford it, she made the place over into a farm that looked as though it was in the hands of someone who didn't mind hard work and long hours. In the autumn of 1905 she hired a clerk from a store in La Porte to come and undertake some carpentry. He made fresh supports for a rickety shed and barn, put up some stout front fencing, and spent time wondering why the hog pen had a link fence all of six feet tall.

'Pigs can't jump,' he reminded her. 'Why six feet?'

'I like things tidy,' she told him, which was no explanation. But years later, when the hog pen had been changed into a rubbish dump, the story was shown the light of day and men thought they understood. Six feet of chain fence kept out intruders, especially if the hogs were fed a curious meat diet.

While he worked at the Gunness place the store clerk was shown into the basement, which was entered by a trapdoor at the back. In the dark were stoutly made tubs and a wringer and some heavy pieces of furniture, including a table and some chairs. The kitchen, following the pattern of Mattie Altic's particular requirements for her establishment, was in a separate wooden-framed addition to the house proper, and above it was a sleeping and living room for any hired man.

Hired men came and went at intervals. So did other males, as the probing of police and reporters proved. But more came than went, which, to say the least, was rather peculiar.

However, Belle Gunness was a good cook. Most women in the district agreed on that point, and she was no slovenly slut. She worked hard around the house and she kept her children looking neat and well fed, points appreciated in such a rural community. Belle sent them to a Quaker day school and on the Sabbath to Sunday school. She bought them a pony and taught them how to harness it to a small cart so that they could drive themselves to and from the farmhouse. She kept Christmas in the old Norse style, cooking lutfisk and sweet puddings.

There were two Belles, from reports. The farmer's widow who toiled on the place, wielding rake and hoe like a man, and the woman who drove into La Porte in her Sunday best, with diamonds bright against her ear-lobes, to take her place in the rear pew in church.

For a few years after Peter Gunness's death the folks around had the notion that Belle would come to terms with life in a way many women similarly placed had done. They expected to hear she was about to marry one of her hired men. One of them was an elderly Swede, who wrote some of Belle's neighbours harsh letters after some of them had talked out of turn about the comely flaxen-haired widow, an armful for any man, for she was close to twenty stone. But nothing came of that, and nothing came of the respectful courtship paid her by a Norwegian named Colson.

Men arrived from considerable distances to visit the widow who owned the Gunness farm. Their first interest in the place and the woman who owned it had been aroused when they read in their local newspaper:

> 'Rich, good-looking woman, owner of a big farm, desires to correspond with a gentleman of wealth and refinement. Object matrimony.'

Or alternatively:

> 'Wanted—A woman who owns a beautifully located and valuable farm in first-class condition wants a good and reliable man as partner in the same. Some little cash is required for which will be furnished first-class security.'

The advertisements were calculated come-ons for different types of men, the self-important and the cautious, who had one thing in common—money. So after making contact with the willing widow by letter, and receiving an encouraging reply, they packed a bag and started for the farm outside La Porte, where they were welcomed by a woman who could put a good spread of appetizing food on a groaning table and who had a smile that was broad and warm and apparently an outlook on life that allowed some introductory familiarities.

In short, Belle Gunness made herself pleasant to the man with cash in his pocket and credit at the bank. And from accounts given later the big woman with the large robust frame and massive arms could make herself most pleasant when she chose.

Neighbours who watched the procession of well-groomed and well-garbed strangers arriving at the Gunness farm often wondered why none of them apparently stayed. The widow's explanation was a shrug of her large shoulders and the brief explanation that her visitor had gone back. Almost none of them was observed actually going back. One fortunate man who did leave the farm was George Busby. After reading of the fire and the discovery of the bodies under the former hog pen he handed Sheriff Smutzer a bundle of letters which had been written to him by an ingratiating Belle Gunness. He told the sheriff that almost as soon as he arrived he was asked how much money he had brought. He had laughingly said very little, but explained that he had several hundred dollars in the bank and a large well-stocked farm. He was strongly advised to sell farm and stock and come back with his money. His reluctance saved his life.

For by the time Busby's letters were read by Sheriff Smutzer a Colorado prospector named Schultz had erected a Klondyke sluice-box and was 'panning' the ashes in the farm ruins. With a water-wagon drawn up close, he was watched by a crowd offering ribald advice. The old-timer from Colorado worked for a week with a dwindling audience. His sluice-box rattled with the jiggling of some curious cutting implements. It surrendered charred pages from books on anatomy and hypnotism and pieces of human skin and bone. It produced twelve men's watches at a time when the hog pen and rubbish heap had produced the bodies of only eight men. Rings and buckles and scraps of twisted metal came to light when the ashes were floated away.

But old Louis Schultz and his sluice-box didn't find what Sheriff Smutzer and the local coroner wanted—Belle's teeth, which had gold fillings.

This omission in all the debris of death gave Sheriff Smutzer, who was becoming tired of cartoon likenesses of himself in various newspapers, serious pause, for he had arrested a man named Ray Lamphere, a carpenter who had been employed by the widow to mend and make fences. A neighbour had claimed to have seen Lamphere near the farmhouse while it was blazing, and he had, after questioning, been arrested on a charge of arson.

Lamphere's story of his experiences while employed by Belle Gunness were gone over. In the light of discoveries at the burned-out farm since his arrest his claims appeared to have special point.

In his statement he said:

> 'Mrs. Gunness made me a proposal of marriage, and after we had become lovers she said that before the ceremony was per-

formed I must insure my life. This I did, making a will in her favour. But somehow, once she got the will, she kept postponing the marriage. Then one day I found a strange man in the house. It was Andrew Helgelien. They thought themselves alone, but I heard my mistress say she was tired of having Lamphere around and intended to get rid of him. Late one afternoon she sent me to the station to meet her cousin, a Mr. Moo. She told me that if he did not arrive I was to stay in town overnight. I met the train at Michigan City, but there was no Mr. Moo on it. I knew then that Mrs. Gunness had concocted the story to get me out of the way. I at once returned to La Porte, and when it was getting near to midnight I stole out to the farm. In the yellow light from a stable lamp I saw Mrs. Gunness bending over a hole in the ground. I walked up to a wire fence around the yard and saw she was sprinkling lime on a dead body. Suddenly she seemed to feel that someone was watching her, and turning she gasped, "My God! I thought you were a ghost." I did nothing but stepped through the gate. Helgelien's head lay staring up at me from the grave. The body was in a gunny sack and the arms and legs had been tossed in upon it. I helped Mrs. Gunness to fill up the hole. From that night I had her in my power.'

Revelationary if it were true, and it sounded true enough, but did it mean Lamphere had been an accomplice in murder?

The police continued to hold him. His father was Squire William Lamphere, who had been a justice of the peace until he began to drink his way to ruin. He had been walking along a street in La Porte one day when he was confronted by a big blonde woman with a wide red smile who said: 'I've been watching you. I want you to come and work for me.' Lamphere had gone to the farm and dumped his things in the hired man's room over the kitchen. The first night he was awakened by a figure in a long pale nightgown decorated with a good deal of embroidery. It was the widow, and she smelled of freshly applied perfume.

'Move over,' she said.

So Lamphere obediently moved over.

But the carpenter and handyman had terrible fits of jealousy when the stream of prospective suitors arrived at the farm. Those were the nights he slept alone. There were other nights when he had little rest and assuredly no pleasure. They were the nights when he knew a suitor had been taken to the room where Belle Gunness kept her chloroform bottle. It was the bedroom reserved for visitors. It was always kept locked, and it was Belle Gunness who guarded the key.

A girl named Anna Brogiski was for a time employed at the farmhouse. She told the police she had never been allowed to go inside the bedroom opening from the parlour. The door was kept locked, and the Gunness children were scared of the room and always hurried past the door with heads averted.

'I was told to keep out,' the girl said, 'and I kept out.'

It was Anna Brogiski's father who dug some of the graves in which the victims at the 'murder farm', as the newspapers referred to the Gunness place, were buried.

'I was told by Mrs. Gunness to dig some pits in which to bury rubbish,' he told the sheriff. 'When each one had been filled in she asked me to dig another.'

To this the authorities added another piece of information that Lamphere was able to supply. It was about a room in which she kept a plentiful supply of ice in hot weather.

'It was a kind of mortuary,' was how he described it, 'big enough to hold at least six bodies at a time. She did the dismembering there, the legs, the arms, and the head being severed from the body with an axe or a saw.'

In the months before he was brought to trial, in November, 1908, Lamphere remained in jail, handing out, from time to time, gruesome vignettes about life as he had lived it in the notorious Indiana 'murder farm'. The lapse of those seven months since the night of the fire enabled the authorities to check on various missing men who had made the lonely one-way journey to the Gunness farmhouse. A good many of them were of Scandinavian stock.

For instance, John Moo, Belle's cousin. He turned up around Christmas 1906 at the farm to enjoy Belle's lutfisk and sweet pudding. On Boxing Day he appeared at the bank in La Porte, accompanied by a smiling Belle, and had drawn out eleven hundred dollars.

When the tale of Belle Gunness's male visitors was told one organ of the popular Press called the cousinly Mr. Moo 'the

Christmas Papa'. After drawing out his money from the bank he had vanished.

So had Ole Budsberg four months later, in April, 1907. On the 6th of that month he had, like cousin John Moo, gone to the bank with Belle Gunness and withdrawn eighteen hundred dollars of savings. He and the money had vanished, and when his sons and the bank asked where, Belle Gunness had told them Oregon, which was a long way from Indiana.

Olaf Lindboe was a young man of thirty, just arrived in the States from Norway. He started west, reached La Porte and the Gunness farm, where according to one witness he was seen lifting an old privy from its hole, and disappeared. He reappeared on May 6th, 1908, when diggers at the burned-down farm found a soft patch of earth at the rear of the pig pen, not far from where Jennie's corpse had been uncovered. He had changed a good deal since an axe had bitten into his skull, but his strong teeth and some of his fair hair remained.

Henry Gurholt was another who vanished to come back when the diggers uncovered his grave. In another uncovered pit that had been filled with rubbish at the back of the hog pen were found the bones of three dead men and the skulls of two. Short dark hair covered the skulls and one had a beard. The one that was razor-clean was Gurholt's.

John Moo's brother turned up and among other relics was shown a watch Ray Lamphere said Belle had given him. When the mourning Moo saw it he said: 'Now I know John's dead for sure. This is his watch, and this is the leather chain he always wore with it.'

Ten bodies were found planted in the ground under that grisly hog pen and rubbish dump. A number were never identified. For instance, who was the young man with only one wisdom tooth and no others in his upper jaw? Who was the man with a hernia, to whom the right-side truss had belonged?

Brogiski, the Polish labourer, admitted digging many of the pits during a hot summer in 1907. That was when Abraham Phillips of West Virginia told relatives he was going to marry a rich Indiana widow. He left home with a pocket-book stuffed with money, a diamond ring on his finger, and a watch. A similar watch to his was one of those found by the diggers. It was the summer

John E. Bunter of McKeesport, Pennsylvania, talked of marrying a widow in Indiana and later left only to vanish; when Tonnes Peter Lien sold his farm after reading an advertisement and left Rushford, Minnesota, with a thousand dollars sewn into the lining of his sleeve to reach La Porte in the expectation, according to his brother, of marrying Mrs. Gunness; when Emil Tell left Osage City, Kansas, with five thousand dollars, on his way to marry a rich widow in La Porte; when E. J. Thiefland of Minneapolis, after corresponding with Belle Gunness, wrote his sister that he was leaving for La Porte 'to see if this lady is on the square'; when S. B. Smith and Paul Ames vanished, to be recalled when a couple of rings, one inscribed S.B., the other P.A., were found later in the charnel pits. Almost incidental to these men who had answered the lush widow's tempting advertisements were other victims, like George Berry, who had in July, 1905, told his family he was off to work for Mrs. Gunness. He took fifteen hundred dollars with him, and joined Gurholt in one of Brogiski's pits.

Christian Hinkley sold his Wisconsin farm for two thousand dollars and took the money to La Porte, while Herman Konitzer took five thousand and Charles Neiburg only five hundred. All three disappeared with their money.

Young Olaf Jensen wrote his mother in Norway in May, 1906, that he had visited a lady who had put a matrimonial advertisement in the *Skandinaven*, and was selling up and going to join her with his money. He was twenty-three and very hopeful, but neither his youth nor his hopes saved him from the chloroform and axe treatment, and he joined the others in the muck under the hog pen.

However, it was Asle Helgelien from Mansfield, South Dakota, brother of the dead Andrew, who revealed how determinedly the butcheress of La Porte had sought victims with money. He had the letter his brother received from her dated September 2nd, 1906, in which she wrote:

'Dear Friend,

Many thousand thanks for both your letter and photograph card. I have read the letter many times and studied the picture much also. I have now so much confidence and interest in our correspondence, especially when I know that you are such an understanding and good Norwegian man. I long so to know you better, but I will try to wait with patience until you get ready up there. I think it will be best that you get everything ready before you come, so you will not have to go back, as it is so far and it will probably be late in the fall. When you once get here I know I will not be alone again. How pleasant it will be to sit and talk Norwegian about everything. Don't you think so, too?

I would enjoy seeing all your beautiful horses, as I am much interested in horses and other critters. Could you not bring with you a pretty young driving horse? It would give us so much pleasure. I have only three horses, which is enough for us, but one could always use two more.'

Then she went on to give some practical advice, which if taken would speed up the departure from South Dakota, and added some additional enticements:

'In regard to your critters, you could take them with you to Chicago if you cannot sell them up there, and the same with the horses. If you will hire a railroad car you can take all of them that you want with you. I am quite sure that you can get very good prices in Chicago. If you thought it would be too lonesome to stay there alone until you sold out, and have no other company, I could come to you and stay with you until you are through. I am well known around there because we lived there for a while. Both of us could then look around a little.

When you are all through and come here, then we must have some good cooking; but take everything with you and say good-bye to Dakota, so you can be here with us. Then you will see how happy we will be, but do not tell a word to anybody up there before you go, but only tell them after you have been here a while.'

The purpose of this last suggested precaution was grimly patent to Sheriff Smutzer when he read the letter, which continued:

'You must pardon me for not writing before, but we have been so busy picking apples and pears to send to market. We are well paid for such, as we are so near Chicago.

Yes, I will try and get all the fall work done, just so that when you get ready up there you will not have to return again, as it will be altogether too lonesome. I have now thrown away all the other answers I got and keep all yours in a secret place by themselves. I will show them all to you when you come here, as I prize them so highly; but I prize the writer more highly, and when I get to know you I will set the writer above all others, as such a man I have not found among the Norwegians in America. There is altogether too much cunning and humbug in this land. Honesty, sincerity, and righteousness last the longest. Where they are found on both sides, then everything will be all right.

I have told you of everything as it really is, and this you will find when you come. You can be sure that you are heartily welcome. Well, I must close for this time and go and milk. Hope soon to hear from you.

From your friend,
Bella Gunness'

As one chronicler of the La Porte thriller has pointed out, the widow proved herself a marathon letter-writer. Andrew Helgelien was a slow starter in the matrimonial stakes. To get him to the tape he was sent a letter every week for sixteen months, and once he found enclosed a four-leaf clover. It was corny but lucky—but not for him.

He eventually arrived in La Porte after setting out from South Dakota on New Year's Day, 1908. A short while later he drew out all his money, which had been placed to his credit in the La Porte bank. Belle Gunness was her old smiling self at his side as he arrived and collected the cash.

She must have had a shock when she had a letter from Asle asking about his brother Andrew, but she was more than equal to the occasion, as witness the familiar exhortation in the second part of her grieving letter in reply:

'It is with tears flooding my eyes and a heart over-whelmed with grief that I write you about your dear brother, my sweetheart. He left my house seemingly happy and since that time I have not seen him. I will go to the end of the world to find him. I love him and will help you.

Sell off everything he owns; get together as much of your own money as you can and come here. We will then go and seek him. Do not neglect to bring the money in cash. I will be ready to go when you arrive.

Yours in great sorrow,

Bella Gunness'

Asle lived to unmask the 'Mail Order Circe', as revealed in her letters to his brother, because he did not take her advice. But time was running out, she must have felt, and made her preparations for decamping before too many suspicions were aroused, and before Ray Lamphere opened his mouth. However, she worked at her mail order offers until shortly before the fire, and possibly the luckiest man in the United States when the news of the terrible discoveries was published was Carl Peterson. He too had received a reply when he had answered one of her advertisements. It was dated April 14th, thirteen days before the fire on the night of 27–28th.

She wrote:

'There have been other answers to the same advertisement. As many as fifty have been received. I have picked out the most respectable, and I have decided that yours is such. My idea is to take a partner to whom I can trust everything, and as we have no acquaintance ourselves I have decided that every applicant I have considered must make a satisfactory deposit of cash or security. I think that is the best way for parties to keep away grafters who are always looking for such opportunities, as I have had experience of them, as I can prove.

Now if you think that you are able some way to put up a thousand dollars cash we can talk matters over personally. If you cannot, is it worth while to consider? I would not care for you as a hired man, as I am tired of that and need a little rest in my home and near my children. I will close for this time.

With friendly regards,

Mrs. P. S. Gunness'

What made Carl Peterson so lucky was his inability to raise the ante. What kept Joe Maxson alive, the hired man was convinced, was the fact that he refused at first to eat an orange Belle Gunness gave him after dinner that fateful night.

'I'll eat it later,' he said, as he dropped it in his pocket.

'Eat it now,' she said. 'It may be the last treat you get from me.'

For some reason those words made him cautious. He ate the orange when she became really insistent, but he locked his door above the kitchen. Perhaps he was supposed to die in the flames. Had she been able to reach him with an axe his body would have been consumed. As it was he lived, and his evidence helped to fill in the pieces of a veritable jigsaw, but a jigsaw still with some essential pieces missing.

Belle Gunness had vanished with about thirty thousand dollars in cash looted from her victims. Had she really vanished in the flesh, or had the one person who knew her terrible secret, Ray Lamphere, who it seems at this late date most certainly started the fire in the kitchen, as she had told him, destroyed her in order to protect himself?

At Lamphere's trial it could not be proved that Belle was alive or dead. Her head had not been found, with its tell-tale golden teeth. The authorities had to be satisfied with prosecuting Lamphere on the single charge of arson. He was found guilty and sentenced to twenty years' imprisonment.

If he knew any more than he told the police he never divulged it. Perhaps because he couldn't without risking his neck. However, his silence did nothing to detract from the public image of the murderous woman who virtually picked him up in La Porte and later gave him instructions how to set fire to Mattie Altic's old house of crude entertainment.

What was the violent urge that compelled Belle Gunness to poison and mutilate and bury her victims under that filthy hog pen?

Perhaps her sister, Mrs. John Larson, had the answer.

'She seemed to change after the death of her first husband,' Mrs. Larson said. 'She became morose and mean. She scraped and saved every penny she could, and even stinted her children of the clothes they needed. Not that she spent the money on herself. She didn't. She simply hoarded it and wanted more and more.'

All the same, that thirty thousand dollars, missing with Belle Gunness, ended up somewhere, and it is hard to believe that it should today be classified as buried treasure.